AMERICAN HISTORY

VOLUME V: WARS OF THE COLONIES

JACOB ABBOTT

SANDYCROFT PUBLISHING

American History Vol. V: Wars of the Colonies

By Jacob Abbott

First published 1863

This edition ©2014

Sandycroft Publishing

http://sandycroftpublishing.com

ISBN 978-1500601874

CONTENTS

CHAPTER IV

WAR WITH KING PHILIP

CHAPTER V

THE LAKES AND THE MISSISSIPPI

CHAPTER VIII
George Washington

CHAPTER IX
The Conquest of Canada

CHAPTER X
Pontiac

LIST OF ENGRAVINGS

PREFACE

It is the design of this work to narrate, in a clear, simple, and intelligible manner, the leading events connected with the history of our country, from the earliest periods, down, as nearly as practicable, to the present time. The several volumes will be illustrated with all necessary maps and with numerous engravings, and the work is intended to comprise, in a distinct and connected narrative, all that it is essential for the general reader to understand in respect to the subject of it, while for those who have time for more extended studies, it may serve as an introduction to other and more copious sources of information.

The author hopes also that the work may be found useful to the young, in awakening in their minds an interest in the history of their country, and a desire for further instruction in respect to it. While it is doubtless true that such a subject can be really grasped only by minds in some degree mature, still the author believes that many young persons, especially such as are intelligent and thoughtful in disposition and character, may derive both entertainment and instruction from a perusal of these pages.

Interior of the blockhouse.

WARS OF THE COLONIES

CHAPTER I
THE THIRTEEN COLONIES

Subject of the Volume

The time required for the complete occupation of the Atlantic seaboard of North America by emigrants from Europe, and the final organization and settlement of all the communities thus formed, as colonies subject to the British crown, may be considered as extending over a period of about fifty years. The commencement of the settlements took place between 1610 and 1620, and it was not until between 1660 and 1670 that New Amsterdam was taken from the Dutch, and the organization of the whole territory under British rule was completely effected.

The duration of the colonial system thus established—extending as it did from the period of its complete organization, in or near 1670, to the time when the differences with the mother country which terminated in the revolution first began to grow serious, which was about 1770—may be considered as occupying a period of about one hundred years. It is the general history of this second period, and especially of the wars and commotions which occurred in the course of it, to interrupt the peaceful avocations of the settlers, and impede the progress of the colonies in wealth and population, which forms the subject of the present volume.

Number of the Colonies

The number of colonies as finally and permanently organized was thirteen. The following is a list of them, with date of the first settlement of each:

Virginia	1607
New York	1614
Massachusetts	1620
New Hampshire	1623
New Jersey	1624
Delaware	1627
Maryland	1633
Connecticut	1635
Rhode Island	1635
North Carolina	1650
South Carolina	1670
Pennsylvania	1682
Georgia	1733

It will be seen by the above table that the first settlement of all these colonies is not strictly comprised within the limit of the fifty years above referred to, Virginia having been occupied a few years before the commencement of it, and Pennsylvania and Georgia not until after the close of it. We can, however, say in general terms that the original colonization of the country occupied about fifty years, and that the colonial condition thus established endured afterward for about a hundred years.

RECAPITULATION

Before entering upon the history of this latter period, it will be well to enumerate these colonies once more, and briefly to recapitulate the circumstances under which they were severally founded, and the condition they were in at the time when the narratives of the present volume begin.

VIRGINIA, 1607

The first settlement was made by a somewhat wild company of adventurers under the leadership of the celebrated John Smith, who is called the father of Virginia. Smith was induced to embark in the undertaking by the representations of Gosnold, who had previously made a voyage to the coast of New England, and had attempted unsuccessfully to found a colony there. Gosnold accompanied Smith in the expedition to Virginia. The first settlement was at Jamestown. The colonists encountered very great difficulties for the first few years. They quarreled among themselves and they quarreled with the Indians around them, and the whole colony was repeatedly reduced to the greatest extremity for want of food. At one time the little remnant that was left actually embarked for England but they were met, on the way down the river, by vessels coming in with supplies, and were persuaded to return.

At length, however, the colony began to take root, and the settlement extended beyond Jamestown to various points on the banks of the neighboring rivers.

In a very short time after the first settlement of the colony, a Dutch vessel came in bringing about twenty African slaves, which were sold to some of the wealthy colonists. This was the origin of the vast system of American slavery, which has since been the cause of so much sorrow and crime.

Notwithstanding the sowing of this terrible seed, however, the colony increased and prospered. It was ruled by a governor appointed by the British crown, and by a legislative assembly elected by the people.

NEW YORK, 1614

There was a dispute from the very commencement, between the English and Dutch governors, in respect to the right to establish colonies at the mouth of the Hudson River. Sebastian Cabot, who was an English navigator, first explored the general line of the coast, while Hendrick Hudson, who, as the Dutch claimed, was then in the service of the Dutch East India Company, was the discoverer of the river, and the first to enter it. The Dutch Company were at that time often sending expeditions to the American coast, to fish for cod along the shores, and to buy furs and skins of the Indians, and at last they began to build huts on the land at the mouth of the Hudson. The English government denied their right to do this and remonstrated with the Dutch government, and many negotiations and much discussion ensued. Nothing was, however, positively settled, and in the meantime the Dutch settlement, which was called New Amsterdam, increased and gradually became a flourishing colony, which extended far into the interior and along the coasts of Long Island Sound, and thence up the Connecticut River, where at length their outposts came into collision with branches of the Massachusetts colonies, which likewise by this time had begun to extend into the Connecticut region, and to form considerable settlements there.

A great deal of difficulty grew out of these collisions, but still the English government were unable to restrain the New Amsterdam colony without going to war with Holland, which for a long time it would have been impolitic for them to do. At length, however, the state of things in Europe changed so that the objections on the part of the English to a war with Holland were removed, and then the whole country of the Hudson was granted formally to the Duke of York, and he was authorized to fit out an armed force to go and take possession of it. This he accordingly did. The Dutch governor, when the English ships appeared, found that he had not force enough to resist them, especially as the people of the colony, consisting as they did in a large proportion of English settlers, seemed not at all disposed to aid him. He accordingly surrendered, and with the troops under his command embarked for Holland; and thus the colony with all its dependencies was transferred to the English crown. The name of the chief settlement was changed at the same time from New Amsterdam to New York, in honor of the duke to whom the territory had been granted. This name it has ever since retained.

MASSACHUSETTS, 1620

The first settlement made in the territory, now included within the limits of the state of Massachusetts, was that of Plymouth, which was established by a company of religious men, the members principally of a church which had been driven from England some years before, and had taken refuge for a time in Holland, but had at length determined to emigrate to America in order to found an entirely new state, in which they might be at liberty to carry out in full their religious views without any hindrance or restraint. They came out in a vessel called the *Mayflower*—about one hundred in number—and after undergoing indescribable hardships and privations, they finally, in the course of a few years, succeeded in establishing a flourishing colony.

In the meanwhile many hunting and trading expeditions were sent out from time to time to the coast of New England from Great Britain, and various landings were made at different points in Massachusetts Bay. The parties engaged in these enterprises at length combined their interests and founded what was called the colony of Massachusetts Bay—the seat of which was the country in the vicinity of Boston. These new settlements soon began to surpass the Plymouth colony in population and wealth. The two communities, however, remained distinct from each other for more than half a century, but at length, in 1692, they were united under a new charter granted by the English government, and the colony of Massachusetts was thus finally organized.

NEW HAMPSHIRE, 1623

The first permanent settlement in New Hampshire was founded by Ferdinando Gorges, in 1623. Gorges was a celebrated merchant adventurer and navigator in those days, and he had been for several years before this time interested in expeditions to the northern part of the North American coast. The principal object of these expeditions was the exploring of the harbors, bays, and river-mouths along the coast, with a view to finding convenient stations for those engaged in the cod fishery, and also for buying corn and other provisions of the Indians for the use of the fishermen, and furs and skins to take home to England. The fur-bearing animals in all this region, which was at that time almost an unbroken forest, were extremely numerous, and on account of the length of the winters and the severity of the cold the furs which they bore were very fine and full, and of excellent quality.

Gorges accordingly, and other adventurers of this class, undertook frequent voyages to these coasts, and in the course of them made many temporary encampments on the land, and even attempted permanent settlements in some cases. One was commenced at the mouth of the Kennebec, in what is now the state of Maine, but it did not succeed. At length in 1622, Gorges, in company with a personage named John Mason whom he associated with, obtained from the Plymouth Company—which was a company composed of wealthy English merchants and other persons of distinction in England, who had obtained from the government the right of control over all attempts at establishing settlements on any part of the coast of New England—a grant of that portion of the territory lying between the Merrimac and the Kennebec, and in the following year, that is in 1623, they sent over a company of colonists who entered the river Piscataqua, and made a settlement on the banks of that river, near where the town of Portsmouth now stands.

After this, other settlements were made within this district, particularly one at Saco and another at Portland. After a few years, however, the territory was divided into two provinces. The western part was assigned to Mason, and he gave to it the name of New Hampshire, in honor of his native county in England. Gorges, who took the eastern half, named his for the same reason New Somersetshire. The government of this latter province was afterward transferred to Massachusetts, and the name was changed to Maine. The province of Maine accordingly did not constitute a separate colony, but remained united with Massachusetts till long after the revolution.

The district assigned to Mason, which received the name of New Hampshire, became at once an independent colony, and settlements branching from it spread rapidly into the interior.

NEW JERSEY, 1624

The territory of New Jersey, as will be seen by the map, lies closely contiguous to New York, and, as might naturally be supposed, the Dutch settlement at the mouth of the Hudson, as soon as it became firmly established and began to spread into the interior, sent out branches in this direction as well as in others. It was about the year 1624 that the first permanent occupation of the soil of New Jersey took place. A few years afterward a company from Sweden and Finland came over and founded a more extended settlement on the banks of the Delaware, having purchased a large tract of land from the Indians for this purpose. When, at length, New Amsterdam was taken by the English, all these settlements, as well as those on the Hudson, fell into the hands of the Duke of York, the whole territory having been granted to the duke by his brother the king.

Situation of the MIDDLE STATES

The territory now forming the state of New Jersey was afterward granted by the Duke of York to other proprietors, having first, however, been divided into two portions, which were called East Jersey and West Jersey. The whole region was often designated as "The Jerseys," even down to quite recent times. The government of the two Jerseys passed through a great many changes, and was all the time more or less dependent upon that of New York, for nearly a hundred years. But at length the two provinces were united and constituted into a distinct and independent colony under the name of New Jersey.

DELAWARE, 1627

The state of Delaware takes its name from Lord de la Ware, who was one of the earliest governors of Virginia. In one of the expeditions which he made along the coast he discovered and entered the great bay lying north of the Chesapeake and gave it his name. The relative situation of the two bays will be seen by the map on the preceding page. There were several attempts made after this to settle the country, one for example by the Dutch, and another, more successful, by the Swedes and Fins. The colony established by these last was known for a time by the name of New Sweden, and the settlements extended into the territory now belonging to Pennsylvania. The Dutch remonstrated against the right of the Swedes to occupy this country, and after a time hostilities broke out between the Swedish colony and that of the Dutch at New Amsterdam. In the end the Swedes were beaten, and all the settlers who would not transfer their allegiance to the conquerors were sent back to Europe.

When, at length, New Amsterdam and with it the whole domain of the Dutch in North America fell into the hands of the English, and after some delay and many disputes among the different proprietors who claimed under grants from the Duke of York and from the English government, in respect to their several boundaries, the colony of Delaware was at length definitely organized and established. For many years, however, it was attached to Pennsylvania, and was under a common government with that colony, as will appear more fully in the sequel.

MARYLAND, 1633

The territory surrounding the headwaters of Chesapeake Bay was granted by King Charles I to George Calvert, Lord of Baltimore, which was an Irish title. He was a Roman Catholic, and a man of considerable wealth and distinction. He first attempted to establish a settlement in Newfoundland, and expended a large sum of money in the undertaking, but at length his little colony was taken from him by the French, and King Charles, by way of compensating him for his loss, made him this grant of the territory around the headwaters of the Chesapeake.

He himself died before he could make arrangements for settling his new domain, and, indeed, before all the formalities of the grant were properly fulfilled, but his brother, Cecil Calvert, inherited his titles and estates, and the grant was finally completed in his name. He immediately took measures for sending out a colony. He was a Roman Catholic like his brother, but had evinced a very liberal spirit in laying the foundations of the future state, for the rights of citizenship and eligibility to office were extended to all Christians of every denomination without distinction. Still nearly all of the first party of colonists were of the same persuasion with himself, and many of the principal families of the state and a large proportion of the population remain of that faith to the present day.

The first company of colonists consisted of about two hundred persons. Lord Baltimore did not come out himself with this colony, but sent a third brother, Leonard Calvert, whom he appointed governor. The name Maryland was given to the colony in honor of the queen of Charles I, whose name was Henrietta Maria.

The Baltimore family held and exercised a species of sovereignty over the colony down to the period of the revolution. The representative of the family for the time being, appointed the governors and approved or disapproved all laws passed by the assembly.

CONNECTICUT, 1635

There were two colonies originally established in Connecticut which were for some years entirely independent of each other. The first was formed by a company of emigrants from Boston and the vicinity, who went across the country to the westward until they reached the Connecticut River, and there laid the foundations of the towns of Windsor, Wethersfield, and Hartford. The Dutch from New Amsterdam had previously built forts and trading houses on the river, and the conflicting claims of the Dutch and the English to the possession of the territory led to much dispute and dissension, which continued for several years, and was not finally determined until New Amsterdam was taken by the expedition sent out by the Duke of York, and the claims and pretensions of the Dutch in respect to the whole country were extinguished forever.

The other Connecticut colony was established at New Haven. The first settlers were a party of emigrants from England, who came out under the charge of two ministers, and their special object was to establish a civil community on a plan of the most strict and literal conformity with the pattern set up, as they supposed, for the imitation of mankind, in the Holy Scriptures. They accordingly made the laws of Moses the basis of their system, and followed them as closely as possible in the enactments which they made for their new state. This system was for a while very strictly persisted in, but after a time it was gradually changed for one more consonant to the ideas and the wants of the present day.

The two Connecticut colonies remained separate and distinct for a number of years. The one was called the colony of Connecticut and the other the colony of New Haven. The colony of Connecticut at length in 1665 sent out an agent to England to procure a charter from the king, not being satisfied with the tenure on which they had up to that time held their territory and jurisdiction. This agent was Mr. Winthrop. He happened to have in his possession a remarkable ring which was given to his grandmother by Charles I. Charles II was then upon the throne, and Winthrop, pending his negotiations for a charter, gave the king this ring. The king, who was a very gay and frivolous man, was so much pleased with the ring that he at once granted the charter, and included within it the colony of New Haven; and thus the colony of Connecticut was definitively organized under the form which it continued to retain down to the Revolution.

RHODE ISLAND, 1635

The first settlement of Rhode Island was the result of a religious dissension in the colony of Massachusetts Bay. The leader of the dissentients was Roger Williams, a minister of great ability and of very ardent piety, but so extremely decided and so uncompromising in his views, that wherever he went his ministrations soon had the effect of raising up a party opposed to the general sentiment of the community on certain points both of theology and of government; and the views which he and his followers maintained were advanced by them in so aggressive a spirit as to lead to the most violent and angry discussions. There is no doubt that Roger Williams was perfectly honest and conscientious in taking this course, while on the other hand, the church authorities in the various towns where he preached, and the magistrates of the colony were perhaps equally conscientious in opposing him. After a long contention and much difficulty Roger Williams was brought to trial, and a sentence of banishment was passed upon him. The intention of the magistrates was to send him to England, but he contrived to escape into the interior of the country and thus to evade their design. He spent the winter among the Indians, and in the spring found his way across Narragansett Bay, and there being joined by a number of his followers from the different towns where he had preached, he laid the foundations of Providence. This was in 1635.

A very few years later another party left Massachusetts under somewhat similar circumstances, and settled on the island in Narragansett Bay, known as Rhode Island. These two settlements remained for a long time distinct, and were known respectively as the *Providence and the Rhode Island Plantations*. At length, during the reign of Charles II, a charter was granted, which included the whole territory under one jurisdiction, and which continued in force as the only written constitution, first of the colony and afterward of the state, down to a very recent period.

NORTH CAROLINA, 1650

The very first attempts of any European power to establish colonies in North America were made on the coast of North Carolina, which was then included with all the territory south of it, to the Gulf of Mexico, under the name of Florida. These attempts were made in 1586 and 1587. A colony was left on the River Roanoke, but when the place was next visited by European ships no remains of the settlement and no traces of the fate of the colonists could be found. The first *permanent* settlement was made in 1650 by a party of emigrants from Virginia, who were induced to leave the mother colony by religious dissensions which there occurred.

In 1661, ten years after the Virginia party entered the territory, a company from Massachusetts arrived, and established a settlement

11

on the banks of Cape Fear River. The settlers had a great deal of difficulty with the Proprietors as they were called, that is wealthy and powerful men in England who claimed to hold the whole territory under grants from the English kings, and at one time these proprietors attempted to introduce the English aristocratic system of government over the colony by means of an artificial imitation of the feudal nobility of Europe. The whole plan, however, completely failed, and in the end the English government bought out the proprietary interest, and the colony came from that time under the control of the crown, and it remained in that condition until the revolution.

SOUTH CAROLINA, 1670

Although the territory of South Carolina at the present day far surpasses that lying immediately to the northward of it, both in wealth and population, it was not occupied by European settlers until a much later period. The wealth of North Carolina depends chiefly upon the vast forests of pine which occupy the ground there, and which produce immense quantities of pitch, tar, turpentine, resin, and other such products, greatly in demand throughout the world for ship-building and other purposes connected with the mechanic arts. The soil of *South* Carolina, on the other hand, consisting as it does in great part of low and rich alluvial tracts, bordering the rivers and the sea, produces at the present day vast quantities of cotton and rice, which are far more valuable than the forest products of the North Carolina plains.

The value of these lands, however, for such purposes, was not at all understood in those early days, and thus the territory, though really more valuable, was long neglected, partly doubtless on account of its being more remote from the mother colony of the south, namely Virginia.

It was not until 1670, more than fifty years after the first settlement was made in Virginia, that any attempt was made to take possession of what is now the territory of South Carolina. A small party from England, under the leadership of William Sayle, arrived during that year on the coast, and made choice of the harbor of Port Royal for their first settlement. They continued to occupy the lands in that vicinity for some years, though their numbers were gradually reduced by sickness and want until at length, in 1680, those that remained concluded to abandon that locality, and to remove to a point of land at the confluence of the Ashley and Cooper rivers, where they commenced a settlement and laid the foundations of the present city of Charleston.

For a time these settlers were left pretty much to themselves, but the whole country which is now comprised within the limits of North Carolina, South Carolina and Georgia had been granted twenty years before by the king to one of the English nobles, Lord Clarendon, and his agents soon after this organized a provincial government over the whole district within which settlements had yet been commenced, the whole district being designated as Carolina. This was a name which had been given to that part of the coast some years before by the French, in honor of the then reigning French monarch, whose name was Charles.

Thus North and South Carolina were for a long time one. It was not until 1719, in fact, that they were separated.

The cultivation of rice, now one of the most important staples of the country, was first introduced by one of the governors of the colony, who had the sagacity to perceive how well adapted the low and marshy districts which abound on the coast were to the cultivation of that plant. Indeed, there was a species of wild rice, which was much used by the Indians, that was indigenous to the country, and had grown there from time immemorial. Cotton was also introduced, but cotton was in those days of comparatively little value for want of some easy mode of separating the fibers from the seed. The object of the cotton fiber, according to the intentions of nature, would appear to be, like that of the down upon the thistle, or the little parachute attached to the dandelion seed, to assist in conveying the seed, by the help of the winds, away from the parent plant to some place where it might have room to grow. Of course, as it has thus to carry the seed, it is firmly attached to it, and the separation of it, in order to get the fiber by itself for the purpose of manufacture, was always a matter of great difficulty until, at length, the cotton gin was invented, a simple machine by which vast quantities of the fibers and seeds are separated from each other in a very rapid and easy manner.

This discovery made the cultivation of the cotton plant an eager object of pursuit in every country where it would grow, and has vastly increased the wealth and population of the cotton growing states of America, among which South Carolina has taken a very prominent position.

PENNSYLVANIA, 1682

The case of Pennsylvania furnishes another example of a colony, the settlement of which was long delayed, but which afterward attained a very high rank among her sisters, both in wealth and population. The chief reason why this territory remained so long unoccupied seems to have been that it lies in the interior, and is thus not so easily accessible from sea. The parties of Swedes and Finns that have already been spoken of as having attempted to colonize the shores of Delaware Bay and river, in the territory now comprised within the limits of the states of Delaware and New Jersey, perhaps extended their settlements in some degree into what is now Pennsylvania, but there was no fixed and permanent occupation of the soil until the year 1682, when King Charles II granted the whole tract to William Penn, in payment of a debt due to Penn's father.

William Penn belonged to a family of considerable distinction, his father having been an admiral in the royal navy, and yet his object in obtaining this grant was very similar in its nature, to that of the poor Pilgrims who planned the settlement at Plymouth sixty years before, namely to escape from religious persecution, and to found a community where men of his persuasion, namely, that of the Society of Friends, commonly called Quakers, could carry out their religious ideas, both in respect to faith and to practice, without hindrance or molestation.

Penn himself had suffered a great deal from persecution in the course of his life. He joined the Society of Friends when he was quite young.

One of the preachers of that persuasion said to him one day, in reference to the trials which he, that is Penn, was suffering on account of his religious views, "There is a faith which overcomes the world, and there is a faith which is overcome by the world." This sentiment made a very strong impression on Penn's mind, and he resolved that *his* faith should be of the conquering and not of the conquered kind. He suffered a great deal both from his family and from the government. His father, who seems to have been as blunt and rough as sailors are generally supposed to be, turned him out of doors several times, and he was repeatedly imprisoned by the public authorities. He bore all, however, with so patient and submissive a spirit that he vanquished his enemies in the end, and came at last to be universally respected and esteemed. His father became fully reconciled to him before he died. He left him a large fortune, and took leave of him with these words, "Son William, let nothing in this world tempt you to wrong your conscience. So will you keep peace at home, which will be a feast to you in the day of trouble."

The general estimation in which Penn was held at this time of his life was such that when he began to take measures for founding his colony, the public was prepared to regard any proposals which he might make with great favor. The proposals themselves too, which he did make, were such as greatly to increase the public confidence in his enterprise. He drew up what he called the FUNDAMENTAL CONSTITUTION of Pennsylvania; and also a FRAME OF GOVERNMENT, in which were embodied the plans and principles on which the new colony was to be founded. The constitution allowed the utmost liberty of conscience in respect to religious faith and worship, and in all other respects was conceived in a very liberal spirit. A large number of families were ready to join the first expedition, which, after crossing the Atlantic, landed on the shores of the Delaware and laid the foundation of Philadelphia.

Penn himself visited his colony soon afterward and made very excellent arrangements while there to promote the prosperity of the settlements, and the welfare and happiness of the people. The policy which he pursued in respect to the Indian title to the land was not only just but generous, since notwithstanding his grant from the king he would occupy no land until he had first paid the natives a full price for it, according to their estimate of its value for their purposes. In consequence of his pursuing this course, and his inducing the settlers to act on the same principles in all their dealings with the Indians, the colony lived at peace with the natives for many years, while other settlements, both to the northward and southward, were often reduced to the extreme of suffering and distress by Indian wars, and by the ravages of fire and sword and the bloody massacres to which they led.

The colony grew very rapidly in wealth and population, and it remained subject to the proprietary interest which the Penn family held in it until the Revolution.

GEORGIA, 1733

The case of Georgia is somewhat similar to that of South Carolina, that is, although in later times, it became one of the wealthiest and most powerful states, on account of the productiveness of portions of the soil, for the great staples of rice and cotton, the original settlement of it was long delayed. It was, in fact, the very last of the colonies founded by the English on the American coast. The reason of this delay was partly owing to the remoteness of the territory from the parent southern colony on the Chesapeake, and partly on account of the exposure of the territory to incursions from the Spaniards who then held Florida, and who claimed that what is now Georgia was included within the limits of the territory which rightfully belonged to them.

At length, however, in 1733 King George II made a grant of the country to James Oglethorpe, who came over with a company of forty followers and laid the foundations of the city of Savannah. Afterward other companies of emigrants came, and the colony went on very prosperously. It remained under the proprietorship of the Oglethorpe family for many years, but at length the jurisdiction thus exercised was ceded to the crown.

THE THREE FORMS OF COLONIAL GOVERNMENT

Such, in brief, were the circumstances connected with the first settlement and early history of the original thirteen colonies from which the American Union was ultimately formed. These colonies were nearly all in successful operation before the close of the seventeenth century. They were alike in respect to being chiefly peopled from Great Britain, and in being subject to the sovereignty of the British crown. They were very unlike, however, in respect to the system of local government which was established over them. They formed, in respect to the character of this government, three classes, namely, the *Charter* Colonies, the *Royal* Colonies, and the *Proprietary* Colonies.

THE CHARTER COLONIES

The government of these colonies was administered by the colonists themselves, under grants of jurisdiction called *charters*, which were bestowed by the English government. The New England colonies were all of this class. The people chose their own governors, elected their own legislatures, and enacted their own laws—subject in the main only to a general obligation of allegiance to the British sovereign, and even this obligation seems to have been sometimes very lightly felt.

THE ROYAL COLONIES

This class of colonies pertained directly to the British crown, and while they elected their own local legislatures, the governors and other important executive officers were appointed by the king of England. Hence this name of Royal Colonies. Virginia, New York, North and South Carolina and New Jersey were of this clam. Under this system, as might have been expected, many differences and dissensions arose, for the governors being appointed in England and acting under instructions from the English ministry, or from the king, and having a veto on the legislation of the local assemblies, often found themselves compelled to act in opposition to public sentiment in the colonies, and this gave rise in many cases to violent and sometimes to long protracted disputes. These disputes and difficulties grew more and more serious as time rolled on, and the colonies increased in wealth and power, until, at last, after the lapse of a hundred years, they culminated in the American Revolution.

THE PROPRIETARY COLONIES

These were the colonies established by wealthy proprietors to whom grants of territory, *with the jurisdiction included,* had been made by the crown. Maryland, Pennsylvania, and at first North and South Carolina, and East and West Jersey were of this class. This system, however, worked very disadvantageously. The proprietors, under the grants of jurisdiction over their several territories which had been made to them, claimed the right to frame the system of government, and to appoint the chief executive officers, and even to control the legislation. While the settlements in any colony were small, and the people few, they would submit to this, but as soon as the community of settlers began to increase in numbers and wealth, they began to feel their power, and to grow very restive under this domination. It was hard enough for the people of the Royal colonies to submit to this sort of surveillance and control, even from the king— but for the people of the Proprietary colonies, to be thus ruled over by a private family living three thousand miles away, was intolerable. After struggling along through these difficulties for some years, four of the six Proprietary colonies, namely, the two Carolinas and the two Jerseys, were transferred to the crown, and only Maryland and Pennsylvania remained in that condition. The proprietary rights of the Penn and Baltimore families continued undisturbed over these until the Revolution.

CHAPTER II
THE PEQUOT WAR

THE CONNECTICUT INDIANS

The scene of the first serious Indian war in which any of the New England colonies were engaged, was Connecticut, and the Indian tribe with which the settlers came in conflict were the Pequots.

The territory now included within the limits of Connecticut and Rhode Island was occupied in those days by a great number of tribes that were in some sense distinct, though more or less connected with each other by intermarriages among the sachems, and by alliances and leagues of various kinds. These tribes in general lived peaceably, each in its own domain, the people being contented with the plain but honest livelihood which they could obtain through the labors of the men in hunting and fishing, and those of the women and older children in cultivating fields of Indian corn.

THE NARRAGANSETTS

The most wealthy, populous and powerful of these tribes were the Narragansetts. They occupied, as might be inferred from their name, the country about the shores of Narragansett Bay, and the various inlets, sounds and rivers that communicate with it. The soil of their country was fertile, and the waters were very prolific in fish of every kind. So they obtained subsistence easily by peaceful and honest pursuits, and the necessity of devising nets and hooks and other tackle for taking fish, and of making canoes for navigating their waters, and of fabricating weapons for the chase, so stimulated their ingenuity that they seem to have made more progress in such rude arts as Indians can practice than most of the other tribes, and the population which their country supported, in proportion to its extent, was greater than that of the others. In a word, the Narragansett nation was the representative of civilization, refinement and wealth, so far as such marks of progress could have any representative among nations of savages.

THE PEQUOTS

The Pequot Indians seem to have occupied the other extreme of the scale. They were a wild, warlike and desperate race. It has been supposed by some writers that they had not been long in Connecticut at the time when it was first settled by the English, but that they came, some few years before, from their original home on the Hudson, through the Housatonic country into that of Connecticut, fighting their way through and among the native tribes that came in their way,

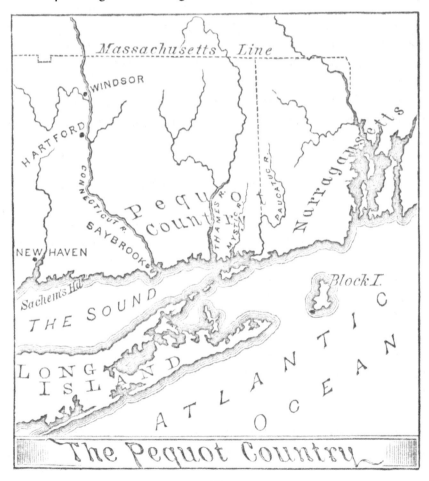

The Pequot Country

until at last they were brought to a stand by arriving at the frontier of the Narragansett country. They accordingly proceeded no farther, but settled down where they were, thus occupying the territory extending along the coast from the mouth of the Connecticut to the neighborhood of the shores of Narragansett Bay.

At any rate, however they came there, there they were when the Dutch and English settlements began to be formed in that country, and all the tribes around them hated and feared them. There was a standing feud between them and the Narragansetts, and the tribes on the Connecticut above them lived in a constant state of uneasiness on account of them. Indeed, it was in consequence of their apprehensions in respect to these Pequots that certain Indian tribes made application to the governors of the Plymouth and Massachusetts Bay colonies to establish an English settlement on the banks of the Connecticut River, which led in part to the first attempt at establishing a colony there. In a very short time after these English settlements began to be formed, the settlers found themselves involved in a war with this people, which became in the end extremely fierce and sanguinary, and ended in the almost utter extermination of the tribe. This war is known in history as the Pequot War. The name of the grand sachem who ruled over the Pequots at this time was Sassacus.

ENGLISH SETTLEMENTS

The map exhibits in a distinct manner the situation of the Pequot country, and its relations to the settlements which had then been commenced by the English. There were three groups of English settlements, or rather three centers in which colonization had been commenced. The principal group was situated on the banks of the Connecticut River, in the northern part of what is now the state, and near the Massachusetts line. The principal settlements were at Hartford and Windsor.

There was, also, near the mouth of the Connecticut, a fort and trading house at Saybrook. This station had just been established by a company from England, and was entirely independent of the settlements up the river.

The third settlement, which had been commenced, was at New Haven.

21

All these settlements were new, having been but very recently undertaken when the war broke out. The little companies of emigrants that occupied them were not, however, so utterly helpless and dependent as the Plymouth colony must have been for some years after it was founded, for they were greatly supported and strengthened by the Plymouth and Massachusetts colonies, which had now become quite strong, and were in constant communication with them.

Besides these English emigrants, the Dutch from New Amsterdam, afterward New York, made frequent voyages up the Connecticut River to trade with the Indians for furs, and they had established several small forts and trading houses at different points along the shores.

The Pequot Country

The Pequot country, as the map shows, extended along the coast from the mouth of the Connecticut toward the shores of Narragansett Bay—being that part of the coast which lies opposite to Block Island and to the eastern end of Long Island. It extended also some distance into the interior. The chief stronghold and usual residence of Sassacus, the grand sachem, was near the mouth of the river Thames, in what is now the town of Groton. It was a strong fort built in the Indian style, and situated on a beautiful eminence commanding a fine view of Long Island Sound, and of the islands off the coast.

Sassacus had another fort farther to the eastward, on the banks of the Mystic River, and all over the country were many little towns and villages occupied by the people of his tribe.

Origin of the Quarrel with the Pequots

Of course the Pequots, being a warlike and an aggressive tribe, accustomed to make their way by fighting for the ground they occupied, would naturally look with great jealousy upon foreigners coming to establish themselves in their neighborhood, and encroaching upon territory belonging, as they considered, exclusively to the Indian race. The English, on the other hand, knowing the character of the Pequots, would look upon them with more suspicion and hostility than upon any other tribes. Indeed, when the other tribes sent messengers to Plymouth and to Boston, to endeavor to ingratiate themselves into the favor of the English and to obtain their friendship and alliance as a means of defending themselves against the Pequots, the English received them in a friendly manner, and evinced a strong inclination to take their part. This gave the Pequots great offence, and confirmed them in their determination to consider the English as their enemies.

Case of Captain Stone and His Party

The first open act of violence which these feelings of secret hostility induced was the destruction by the Indians of a party of trading adventurers under a certain Captain Stone, who went up the Connecticut in his vessel about the time that the English settlements above referred to were forming. This Captain Stone was known to be an unscrupulous and bad man. He came cruising along the coast in his vessel from far to the eastward of Massachusetts Bay, stopping from time to time to trade with the Indians, until finally he entered Connecticut River. The next that was heard of him was that he and all his men had been murdered by the Pequots, and his vessel blown up and burned. The story which came to the colonists and was generally circulated among them was this:

That after Captain Stone had entered the river he sent three men ashore with fowling pieces to see if they could shoot some game—that these men fell into the hands of the Indians who murdered them—that the sachem, a subordinate chieftain who lived on that part of the river, then proceeded along the shore to where the vessel was lying, and went on board, taking with him some of his men and pretending to be friendly—of course concealing the fate of the three men who had gone on shore; that he remained in the cabin until the captain went to sleep, and then, after dispatching the captain by knocking him on the head, the men seized the guns that were there, and made a rush forward on the deck and attacked the crew; that in the fray the powder magazine took fire and blew up a portion of the deck; that the Indians escaped to the shore without injury from the explosion, but immediately afterward returned to the attack and completed their work by burning the vessel and killing all the crew.

This story, of course, greatly excited and alarmed the colonists, but for a time no steps were taken to obtain redress.

The Indian Account of the Affair

The next year, however, the authorities at Boston had an opportunity to hear the Indian account of the affair; for at that time Sassacus sent an embassage to Boston to propose a treaty of friendship and alliance with the English. The messenger carried two bundles of sticks to represent the number of beaver and other skins which the sachem would give. He also carried with him a propitiatory present of wampum. This application led to some negotiations, in the course of which the governor of Massachusetts said he could not make any treaty with the tribe except on condition of their giving up the murderers of Captain Stone. The messengers replied that the sachem who had been chiefly concerned in that transaction had since been killed by the Dutch, and that all the others that had been joined with him, except two, had died of the smallpox. Those two they said they presumed Sassacus would deliver up, if it should appear that they were really guilty.

They said, however, that the Indians acted only in self-defense in the transaction. According to their account Captain Stone, after entering the river, had seized two of the Indians and carried them up the river with him by force, in order to make them act as pilots, and to prevent them from making their escape he kept them bound with their hands behind them. After going up some distance the captain went on shore taking these two men with him, their hands still tied behind them. The other natives, their countrymen, seeing them in this condition naturally desired to rescue them, and in the attempt which they made to do so, the captain and two of his crew who had come on shore with him were killed. Afterward the vessel was blown up and those that remained on board perished, but what the cause of the explosion was they did not know. An explanation was subsequently given by the Indians, as will presently appear, which threw more light on this affair.

TREATY MADE

The authorities in Boston were, on the whole, rather inclined to believe that the Indian version of the affair above related was the most correct one.

At any rate they went on with their negotiations, and pretty soon concluded what may be called a treaty of peace and commerce with the Pequot tribe. This treaty was made and executed at Boston, two Pequot messengers who went there for the purpose representing the Indian sachem. It consisted of only three articles, specifying:

1. That the English were to be allowed peaceable possession of as much land in Connecticut as they should require for their settlements.

2. That in respect to the murder of Captain Stone, Sassacus should pay four hundred fathoms of wampum, forty beaver skins and thirty other skins, by way of penalty for the crime committed by his people, and also deliver up the two remaining murderers whenever the governor of Massachusetts should send for them.

3. That the governor would send a vessel to the Pequot country immediately to trade with them.

WAMPUM

The wampum referred to consisted of long strings of coarse beads made of shells, which served among the Indians the purpose of money. The universal demand for this wampum, as an ornamental portion of the dress, gave to the article a certain intrinsic value as merchandise, which was the foundation of its current value, as money.

Of course to the colonists it was of no direct use, as the wives and daughters of civilized men would only despise a style of ornamentation so barbarous, the wampum having the appearance of strings of coarse and roughly shaped white buttons. Still as the article was everywhere valued by the Indians, furs and skins could be bought of them with it, and thus it became valuable to the colonists as a medium of trade.

Cunning of the Narragansetts

The treaty, when agreed upon, was drawn up in due form and the two Indians signed it by making their marks. The business being thus arranged the Indian embassadors were about setting out on their return home, when the governor of the colony learned by some means that there was a party of Narragansett warriors lying in ambush on the way, at a short distance from Boston, with a view of intercepting and killing them. The story was that there were three hundred Narragansetts in this party, and that they were lurking on the banks of the Neponset River—a small stream which flows along the confines of the town of Dorchester—expecting that the two Pequots would pass that way on their return.

The governor immediately sent a small body of armed men to communicate with this party, and to request the leaders of it to come to Boston and see him. On receiving this message two chieftains, attended by their followers, the number of which as it proved were only about twenty, came to Boston. On being questioned by the governor in respect to their intentions they said that they had been on a hunting excursion about the country, and before returning home they had only stopped at Neponset to make a visit to some friendly Indians living there. Whatever may have been their real designs they were now very willing to promise the governor not to molest the Pequots on their way home, especially as the governor made them a promise, on his part, that if the treaty which they had signed was carried into effect, and the wampum paid, he intended to give a considerable portion of it to the Narragansetts. So the two Pequots were allowed to return home in peace.

New Difficulties

The treaty went into effect and was tolerably well observed for some time as will be seen hereafter—though the Pequots were very slow in making up the amount of wampum stipulated for—until, at length, in 1636 the story came to the colonists that a man named Oldham, who had been trading on the coast, had been murdered at Block Island by some Indians, and that the murderers had gone to the Pequot country and were protected there. Mr. Oldham was an inhabitant of Dorchester, which was a part of the Massachusetts colony, and the governor felt it incumbent upon him to take measures for vindicating the authority of the colony by avenging his death.

THE OLDHAM AFFAIR

The circumstances of the Oldham affair were as follows. The man who had been murdered navigated a small vessel called a pinnace, in which he was accustomed to visit the Indian settlements and trade with the natives for furs and corn. In 1636 he made one of these voyages to the Pequot country, and on his return he stopped at Block Island, which was then inhabited by Indians connected with the Narragansett tribe.

It so happened that the next day after his arrival there, another vessel, commanded by a certain John Gallop, came that way in the prosecution of a similar trading voyage to the Indians on Long Island. When Gallop came near the Block Island shore he saw Captain Oldham's pinnace lying there, with a large number of Indians on the deck, and an Indian canoe, loaded with goods, going from the pinnace toward the shore. He immediately suspected that something was wrong, and he at once ran down toward the pinnace and hailed her in English. He received no answer. He knew by this that the vessel was in the possession of the Indians. He saw, too, that many of them were brandishing guns, and presently the sail went up and the vessel began to move off to the northward, toward the mainland.

He immediately bore up ahead of the pinnace so as to intercept her and then poured in volley after volley of musketry. Many of the Indians were killed and the rest were driven below. Gallop immediately took a little circuit and then came down upon the pinnace so as to strike her with all his force upon the quarter, which gave her such a shock as almost overset her, and frightened the Indians so much that six of them jumped out and were drowned in attempting to swim to shore.

Captain Gallop then bore round and came down upon the pinnace again, giving her another shock, but as no more Indians appeared he began to fire through the sides of the vessel, which were

27

Recapture of the pinnace.

so thin that the bullets easily went through. This terrified the Indians that remained below so much that six more of them rushed up to the deck and leaped overboard into the water, where they sank and drowned.

Captain Gallop had only three men and two boys with him to navigate his vessel, but seeing that so many of the Indians had been disposed of he now ventured to board the pinnace and take possession of her. There were some Indians still below. Two of these came up and surrendered. Gallop attempted to bind them, but finding that he could not conveniently secure them both, he threw one of them into the sea. There were two others that still remained below, and these last were armed with swords and had shut themselves up in the cabin where Gallop could not well get at them. So he fastened them in and let them remain.

On looking about over the deck of the pinnace Captain Gallop found the dead body of Captain Oldham lying under an old sail. The head was split open and the limbs were dreadfully mutilated. Captain Gallop committed the body to the sea, and then proceeded to take off from the vessel all the sails and rigging, and everything else that was of value and could be easily removed. He then took the vessel in tow, in order, if possible, to conduct her to some port—the two Indians still remaining shut up below. The wind, however, began to blow in the night and a heavy sea arose, so that he was obliged to cast off his prize. She went drifting away toward the mainland, and he saw her no more.

DEMANDS OF SATISFACTION

The government of the Massachusetts colony immediately demanded satisfaction of the Narragansetts for this act of murder and robbery. The Narragansett authorities seemed very willing to do all in their power to atone for it. Two Indians and two boys that had been with Captain Oldham in his pinnace, serving as his crew, were recovered and sent to Boston. Ample apologies were made too, and every effort promised to discover and punish the murderers.

This seems to have satisfied the colonists so far as the Narragansett nation was concerned, but it was said that a portion of the murderers of Oldham had escaped to the Pequot territory, and had been harbored and protected there. Accordingly the government of the colony determined to send an armed force to punish first the Block Island Indians for having allowed the crime to be committed in their territory, and then the Pequots for having, as was alleged, harbored the criminals. The person who was to have charge of this expedition was Captain Endicott.

EXPEDITION OF CAPTAIN ENDICOTT

The orders given to Captain Endicott were very severe, not to say unjust and cruel. Indeed, the object of the Massachusetts government was, in the measures which they were about to take, not to do justice, but to execute vengeance—not to inflict upon guilty individuals a punishment which their personal crimes deserved, but to strike terror into the hearts of the whole tribe, by an overwhelming exhibition of the stern and merciless efficiency of English power.

Endicott was to proceed to Block Island, burn and destroy all the Indian villages, and kill all the men that he could find, though he was to spare the women and children. Then he was to proceed to the mainland and there summon the grand sachem to appear. He was to charge the sachem with having harbored the Block Island murderers, and to demand of him the immediate surrender of them, and also of the murderers of Captain Stone, and the payment of the arrears of wampum due, under the former treaty, and four hundred fathoms more, making a thousand fathoms in all. If the sachem found himself unable to deliver up the men and pay the wampum on the spot, then he was to surrender into the hands of Endicott twenty children as hostages, to be held by them until the men and the wampum were forthcoming; and if the sachem refused to comply with this demand, then Captain Endicott was to attack the Indians at once, destroy as many of them as he could, and lay waste the country with fire and sword.

The government of Massachusetts justified this severity by the plea, that in dealing with such savages the only alternative was very rough justice or no justice at all. As all the ordinary modes practiced among civilized nations for examining evidence and distinguishing between the innocent and the guilty were wanting, the only thing to be done was to hold the whole community responsible for the crimes which they allowed individual members to commit. This was moreover in accordance with the settled international law—if we may dignify by that phrase the barbarous usages in force among tribes of savages—which prevailed and was universally acknowledged among the Indians themselves.

Our forefathers too, in those days, drew sometimes something like a sanction for their unsparing severity in dealing with the Indians from the examples set them, in the Mosaic history, by the children of Israel, in extirpating the Pagan aborigines of Canaan. Neither of these excuses seem to us at the present day to justify their proceedings.

Captain Endicott at Block Island

Endicott's expedition consisted of a little fleet of several small vessels and an armed force of ninety men. He reached Block Island at a time when a fresh wind was blowing, and a heavy surf was rolling in upon the shore. There was a single Indian seen walking along the beach. Captain Endicott sent a boat toward the shore with about a dozen soldiers in it. Just as the boat was drawing near the beach a large number of Indians suddenly appeared from behind a range of sand hills, and rushing down to the beach shot a volley of arrows at the men in the boat. One man was wounded in the neck by an arrow which came with such force that it passed through a collar "thick and stiff," they said, "as an oaken board."

The surf was so high that the men deemed it not safe to run the boat to the shore lest it should be stove by striking upon the rocks, and thus the means of retreat to the vessel be cut off entirely from the party landed. They accordingly kept the boat outside the breakers, while the soldiers leaped from it into the water and hurried to the land. The Indians fled from the beach and immediately disappeared from view in the thickets. The soldiers took possession of the vacant ground, and the rest of the force was immediately landed from the vessel. The party encamped for the night and set sentinels. They expected all night to be attacked. They were, however, not disturbed and the next morning the whole force, except such as were necessary to guard the boats and vessels, set off on their mission of destruction.

31

It would be very painful to dwell on the terrible scenes of devastation and slaughter which followed. The soldiers spent two days in ransacking the island in all directions and destroying everything that came in their way. They found two villages, but they were deserted except by the dogs. The English burnt the wigwams, shot the poor dogs, staved and broke to pieces the canoes, laid waste the cornfields, and then went off in all directions around to explore the woods and swamps and hunt out the wretched fugitives who had fled to these secret recesses to save their lives. They could not find a great many of them though the commander reported that they killed fourteen. This, however, may have been only an empty boast, as the Narragansett on the mainland subsequently reported that they only killed one.

THE EXPEDITION TOUCHES AT THE FORT AT SAYBROOK

After finishing this work of devastation the troops were reembarked and the expedition sailed again. Instead of proceeding directly to the mainland, Captain Endicott sailed first for Fort Saybrook, in order to communicate with the garrison there and obtain their cooperation. The commander of the fort at this time was Lieutenant Gardiner. He was greatly astonished when he saw such an armament coming into the harbor, and when he learned what Captain Endicott had done at Block Island and what he intended to do in the Pequot country on the mainland, he remonstrated very earnestly against the whole proceeding. "You have come," said he, "to raise a nest of wasps about our ears, and then you will flee away."

But these remonstrances were unavailing with Captain Endicott. He was determined to proceed; and Lieutenant Gardiner, finding that the work must be done, concluded that it would be better that it should be done effectually, and so he added to the force two shallops and twenty men.

After remaining four days at Saybrook the fleet sailed again, and passing by the mouth of the Connecticut it advanced along the coast toward the mouth of the Thames, on the banks of which river, as has already been said, the chief stronghold of Sassacus was situated.

THE EXPEDITION IN THE THAMES

When the fleet entered the Thames several Indians came down to the shore and began to call out to the ships, to inquire in a friendly manner why they had come with so many vessels, and what they were going to do. To this the English made no reply but went quietly on, up the river.

The Indians began now to be alarmed, and all that night the men on board the ships heard shouts and cries, in tones of distress and fear, all along the shore and in the woods, as if the inhabitants were taking measures to escape from the threatened danger.

A PARLEY

In the morning a boat was seen coming from the shore. It contained an Indian of a tall and majestic form, and of a very imposing carriage and demeanor. He came on board Captain Endicott's vessel and a parley ensued. There was a calm and quiet dignity in the appearance of this Indian and in his words, which greatly impressed those who witnessed the interview.

The Indian asked what was the object of the coming of such a fleet into their river. To this Captain Endicott replied by enumerating the complaints of the English, and demanded the redress which he had been instructed to exact, namely the delivery of the supposed murderers, the payment of one thousand fathoms of wampum, and the surrender of twenty children as hostages to be held until the other conditions should be fulfilled.

The Indian embassador replied calmly and with courtesy to these demands, and he gave now an explanation in regard to the death of Captain Stone, who he admitted had been killed by an Indian on board his vessel, though it will be remembered, that in the first Indian account of the affair this was denied. His statement was, that some time before Captain Stone's voyage, a trading vessel—a Dutch vessel as it afterward appeared—came up the river, and that the captain of it contrived by treachery to get one of their sachems on board, and then called out to the people on shore that if they wished him to be set at liberty again they must pay a bushel of wampum for his ransom. If they would send on board that amount of wampum he would send the sachem on shore.

So the Indians, with great effort, collected that large amount of wampum and sent it to the vessel, and then the captain, by way of keeping his promise, sent the *dead body* of the sachem to them, having treacherously murdered him in the meantime. The vessel then sailed away.

This affair greatly exasperated the Indians, and in accordance with their usages in such cases, in dealing with each other, they determined to kill the first officer of the white men that should come into their country. It happened that Captain Stone was the man upon whom the chance fell—the Indians not making any distinction between the English and the Dutch. Accordingly when Stone's vessel appeared, the son of the sachem who had been murdered went with some others on board the vessel, and there remained drinking with the captain in his cabin until the captain became intoxicated. There was no great improbability in this part of the story, as the captain was known to be a very intemperate and dissolute man, and was in the habit of drinking and carousing with the Indians when he went to trade among them.

As soon as the liquor had produced its effect, the Indians killed the captain with a hatchet, and then attacked the rest of the crew, and in the fray the vessel was blown up and all the sailors perished, though the Indians jumped overboard in season and escaped.

There followed between Captain Endicott and the Indian some discussion on the questions at issue, in which the Indian endeavored, as well as he could, to defend his country. At length the embassador returned to the shore to report the demands of the English, promising to bring back an answer very soon.

LANDING OF THE ENGLISH

But Endicott would not wait for an answer. He immediately proceeded to land his forces and to take up a position on the shore, in martial array. There followed other interviews with different Indians who came around the camp to remonstrate, or to ask for delay, but Endicott was very impatient, and before anything was settled he suddenly ordered all the Indians to begone, telling them that he had come to fight them and was now ready, but he would give them so far a chance for their lives as not to fire upon them till they had time to get once out of the reach of his guns.

So the Indians fled in terror toward the woods while Endicott's men pursuing them immediately commenced hostilities.

The scenes of Block Island were now reenacted in all their horror. The troops spent the day in burning wigwams, wasting cornfields, shooting at every living thing they could see, staving canoes, and destroying every species of property. At night, wearied with their work, they returned on board their vessels. The next morning they landed on the opposite shore of the river, and spent a second day in carrying everywhere the same sweeping destruction on that side. Having thus, as he thought, sufficiently executed his cruel mission, Captain Endicott set sail again for Boston, with all his vessels and all his soldiers safe, except the wound in the neck of one man.

THE PEQUOTS EFFECTUALLY AROUSED

The consequences of such proceedings were exactly what Lieutenant Gardiner had predicted. The Pequots, instead of being overawed and made submissive by these outrages, were only aroused and exasperated by them. They immediately began as one man to prepare for war. The first step that Sassacus took was to endeavor to induce the Narragansetts to join them. For this purpose he sent messengers to the Narragansett country with offers of peace with that tribe, and a proposal that they should make common cause with him against the foreign foe. The Narragansetts were on the point of acceding to these requests, and they would doubtless have done so had it not been for the influence of Roger Williams, who had before this period commenced his settlement in their country, and who had at this time acquired great influence over the chieftains of the tribe. Through his influence the Narragansetts at last decided to take sides with the English, and they sent an embassy to Boston, where a formal and solemn treaty of alliance was made with the Massachusetts colony.

DESPERATE HOSTILITIES OF THE PEQUOTS

The Pequots immediately commenced operations. They sent parties of armed men to prowl about Fort Saybrook, and about all the English settlements on the Connecticut River, and to seize and destroy everything that came within their reach. They captured five men who had been sent out from Fort Saybrook to harvest a field of corn, and who had very imprudently strayed away into the woods, and put them to death with cruel tortures; and then, that night, they came as near the fort as they dared and taunted and defied the garrison by imitating the cries and groans which the five men had emitted in their dying agonies.

A few days afterward another party were sent up the river to a certain island in hopes of cutting and saving some hay there, when the Indians set upon them, and though most of the party escaped, one of them was seized by them and taken off into the woods and there roasted alive.

Another man who went up the river in a vessel was taken prisoner, on landing, and brought down in sight of the fort and there put to death with tortures and mutilations too horrid to be described, in the very view of the garrison, who were too few in numbers to interfere.

In a word, the Indians kept such constant watch about the fort that it was impossible to conduct any operations for tilling the ground or securing crops already grown, or for obtaining food by hunting or fishing. Once or twice Lieutenant Gardiner, finding this state of things intolerable, sent out strong parties of armed men to disperse or destroy these men—but in such cases, though they traversed the woods faithfully in every direction, there was never by any chance a single Indian to be found.

CONDITION OF THE SETTLEMENTS UP THE RIVER

The infant colony up the river was substantially in the same condition with Fort Saybrook. Every settlement was so surrounded and hemmed in by savages prowling about everywhere in the woods, that no one could venture away from his house but at the risk of his life. If the men banded themselves together and went armed to their fields, then in their absence the Indians would attack the villages and carry off the women and girls as captives. Among the captives thus taken were two young girls, who were subsequently rescued and restored to their parents as will appear in the next chapter.

Almost all communication up and down the river was stopped too, for the Indians had full possession of the stream by their canoes. In these canoes they could come out at night from small coves and inlets and attack any vessel attempting to come up, and then could disappear as suddenly as they came. In fine, the progress of all the settlements was completely arrested, and it became plain that unless something effectual could be done to overthrow the Pequot power, the whole region must be abandoned.

APPEAL TO THE GOVERNMENT OF MASSACHUSETTS

Under these circumstances the people of the Connecticut settlements, after full deliberation on the subject, sent an earnest appeal to the authorities of the Massachusetts Bay colony, calling upon them to come to their aid. You, they said, have been the means of bringing this evil upon us by the expedition of Captain Endicott to revenge the death of one of your own people, and now it devolves upon you to rescue us from it.

The Massachusetts people admitted the justice of this claim, and they determined at once to organize an expedition strong enough to break up and destroy the Pequot power once for all—even to the extent, if necessary, of the utter extermination of the tribe.

CHAPTER III
END OF THE PEQUOT WAR

PREPARATIONS FOR THE FINAL STRUGGLE

It was arranged that the different colonies and settlements should furnish each its own quota of troops for the war. The first expedition was to start from Hartford, and was to consist of the quotas furnished by the settlements on the river, namely, Hartford forty-two, Windsor thirty and Wethersfield eighteen, making an army of *ninety* men in all! This was the total number of soldiers which at that time the whole civil population of Connecticut could raise for a war on which the very existence of the people depended. The difference between those days and the present is shown by the fact that the descendants and representatives of these men, living within the same limits, have already, January 1, 1863, furnished nearly thirty thousand men for the war of the Southern rebellion.

INDIAN AUXILIARIES

Besides these ninety Englishmen there were about seventy Indians in the expedition. These Indians were of the Mohegan tribe and were under the command of a chieftain or sachem named Uncas, who lived near where the town of Norwich is now situated. The Mohegans and the Pequots had formerly been connected, and Uncas had been in some sense subordinate to Sassacus; but he had quarreled with him, and rebelled against his authority, and was now easily persuaded to join the English in making war upon him. The English were very distrustful of the fidelity of these Indians, but still they needed them as guides, and they concluded on the whole to risk the chance of taking them.

THE COMMANDER

The expedition was put under the command of Captain John Mason—a military man who had been for some time in the fort at Saybrook. He was a man of tall and commanding appearance, stern in his manners, and very resolute and determined in character.

One of the ministers of Hartford, Mr. Stone, was appointed to accompany the expedition as chaplain.

THE RENDEZVOUS

The troops assembled at Hartford, where they were to embark on board some small vessels provided for the purpose and proceed down the river to Fort Saybrook, at which place they were to make their final preparations for the campaign. From Saybrook they were to proceed along the coast to the mouth of the Thames—which was the maritime entrance to the Pequot territory, and was, in fact, often called Pequot Harbor—and there to commence active operations.

The troops were embarked at Hartford on board a little fleet consisting of a schooner and two or three large sailboats. There were ninety Englishmen and seventy Indians. When all was ready the fleet set sail and proceeded down the river.

THE VOYAGE

The voyage was not very prosperous, for the water was low, and as the vessels were small they were continually running aground. The Indians soon became tired of this kind of navigation, so much inferior, as they considered it, to their mode of paddling about in canoes, which could move in the shallowest water, and which, even if they did at any time run upon a sandbank, could be easily set afloat again by the boatmen leaping into the water alongside, and pushing them off with their hands upon the gunwales. Accordingly after a while the Indians were set on shore in order that they might proceed to Fort Saybrook by land.

ARRIVAL OF THE EXPEDITION AT FORT SAYBROOK

In due time both divisions arrived at Fort Saybrook. The Indians reported that on their way they had encountered a party of Pequots, thirty or forty in number, and had killed seven of them, without any loss on their side except the wounding of one man. This news greatly pleased Captain Mason and the English under his command, as tending to show that their Indian allies were really in earnest and could be relied upon. Lieutenant Gardiner, however, who knew the artfulness of the Indian character, was still very suspicious in respect to their ultimate designs.

"How dare you trust these Mohegans?" said he to Captain Mason. "It is not a year since they were good friends and allies with the Pequots."

"I *am obliged* to trust them," said Captain Mason, "for it is absolutely necessary for me to have them as guides in the Pequot country."

THE INDIANS PUT TO THE TEST

Lieutenant Gardiner was still not satisfied and he determined to put the Indians to a new test. So he called Uncas before him and said to him,

"You say you are going to help Captain Mason in this war. Perhaps it is so, but I wish to have some proof of it. Last night a canoe with six Indians went up the Bass River, and they have not returned. Send twenty of your men and bring me down those Indians dead or alive. If you do this then you shall go with Captain Mason. If not, not."

Uncas accepted this proposal and sent off the twenty men. In due time they returned having killed four of the men and taken one of the other two prisoner. The sixth seems to have escaped.

THE PRISONER KISWAS

The name of the prisoner was Kiswas. He was well known at the fort, having lived there a long time before the war broke out, and having learned to speak English tolerably well. He had appeared very friendly toward the English at that time, but since the commencement of the war he had left the fort and joined his countrymen, and he was able to render them great aid in their hostile operations by his knowledge of the fort, and of the usages and customs of the garrison. Of course the English, though very unjustly, considered him as in some sense a traitor.

DREADFUL FATE OF KISWAS

The Indians, on coming back to the fort with their prisoner, demanded that he should be left in their hands to be tortured to death according to their custom. The English, partly under the exasperation which they felt toward him as a traitor, and also as having been an aider and abettor in all the horrid cruelties which the Pequots had practiced upon the prisoners that they had taken from time to time, and also, perhaps, feeling that if they accepted the services of savages as their allies in the war, they ought to allow them to conduct their portion of the operations in their own way, at once yielded to this demand. The Mohegans accordingly led the unhappy prisoner out to his execution, he daring and defying them all the time, and challenging them to do their worst.

The cruelties which were practiced by the Indians on such occasions are altogether too horrible to be described. In order to give the reader once for all an idea of the inhuman barbarity of these scenes, it may be right to say in this case that the Mohegans fastened their victim to a tree—binding one of his legs securely to the trunk—and then attaching a rope to the other leg, and manning the rope with twenty warriors, they pulled upon it until the body of the wretched man was torn asunder.

One of the English officers who stood by witnessing this scene found it impossible to endure the spectacle, and so he shot the struggling and quivering victim through the head in order to put him out of his misery.

RESCUE OF THE TWO CAPTIVE GIRLS

The English party on their arrival at the fort, to their great joy found there the two girls who have already been spoken of as

41

having been taken captive up the river. They had been rescued by a Dutch vessel and brought to the fort while the English expedition was coming down the river. This Dutch vessel had come from New Amsterdam for the purpose of trading with the Pequots, not knowing of the breaking out of the war. They touched at the fort on their way, and the commander, Lieutenant Gardiner, strongly objected to their going on.

"In your trade with them," said he, "you will supply them with kettles and other articles of metal, and these things will be just what they want to make arrowheads of to shoot at us."

After some altercation on this point the Dutch captain promised that if the commander of the fort would consent to his going on he would redeem the two captive girls, and bring them safe to the fort.

To this Lieutenant Gardiner agreed, and the Dutch vessel proceeded on her voyage.

MANNER IN WHICH THE RESCUE WAS EFFECTED

The vessel entered the River Thames and presently sent a boat on shore with offers to trade with the natives—saying, however, that in return for their merchandise they wanted not wampum or furs, but only the two English girls who were held as captives. Sassacus sent word back that he could not let the captives go.

The Dutch then determined to employ artifice, a means of attaining any desired end that is always unscrupulously resorted to in dealings between hostile or semi-hostile people, and which is called by those who practice it stratagem, and by those against whom it is practiced treachery. They contrived by pretending not to care much about the two girls, and by affecting an unconcerned and friendly demeanor, to inveigle seven of the principal men among the Indians on board their vessel, and then when they had these visitors secure, they called out to the Indians on the bank that if they would send the two girls on board they should have their countrymen again; but if they refused then they would take the men out into the open sea and throw them overboard.

The Indians supposed at first that this was an empty threat, and refused to send the girls. The Dutchman then hoisted his sails and began to proceed down the river. When the Indians found at length that he was in earnest they put the two girls on board two canoes, and sent men to paddle them off at full speed and overtake the vessel. The vessel held back until the canoes came up, and the girls were then exchanged for the seven men, and were brought safe to Saybrook.

The Girls' Account of Their Adventures

Of course the two children were closely questioned about what happened to them during their captivity. They said in answer to these inquiries that the Indians treated them very kindly, and took them about from place to place and showed them all their wigwams and everything that was curious, and endeavored in many ways to amuse them, or as they expressed it, to "make them merry." The Indians had a number of guns, they said, and a little powder and shot, and they were very eager to learn from the girls how the white people made their powder, in order that they might make it for themselves. They asked the girls if they knew how to make it, and when they found that they knew nothing about it they seemed to be much disappointed, and would perhaps have treated the girls with neglect, or even with cruelty, if the wife of a certain chieftain named Mononotto had not taken them under her special protection.

Subsequent Adventures of the Two Girls

The girls were not immediately restored to their parents, for the Dutch governor of New Amsterdam, who it seems knew of the captivity of these children before the Dutch vessel sailed from that port, had given the captain orders to recover them if he could possibly do so, and had also directed that in case they should be recovered they should be brought first to New Amsterdam, in order that he might see and talk with them, hoping probably by their means to obtain some useful information about the condition of the Pequot tribe, the state of the country, and the manners and customs of the people.

Accordingly from Saybrook the children were taken to New Amsterdam where they remained for a time the guests of the governor, and objects of great interest and curiosity to all the town. They were at length put on board another vessel, and sailing along the sound to the mouth of the Connecticut, and thence up that river nearly fifty miles to their home, they were finally restored to their parents safe and sound.

Consultations in Respect to the Plans of the Campaign

When all the preliminaries had been settled, and the time arrived for the expedition to go forward to its work, the proper course to be pursued in advancing into the Pequot territory came up for final decision, and it gave rise to much difference of opinion. The most obvious course would be to sail directly for the Thames and passing up that river to enter at once into the heart of the country. But Captain Mason thought that a better plan would be for them to pass by the Thames and enter the Narragansett country which lay beyond, and then come back into the Pequot country by land, through the woods.

By this means he thought they would perhaps be able to take the Pequots unawares by approaching them from an unexpected quarter. The expedition might, moreover, hope to obtain some reinforcements from the Narragansetts themselves, and thus enter the enemy's country with a larger force.

Some of the other officers, however, and many of the men, were opposed to this plan, thinking it dangerous for them to leave their ships and trust themselves to all the chances of a long and hazardous march through the woods, where they might get lost in the swamps, or fall into ambuscades.

The Prayers of the Chaplain

Under these circumstances Captain Mason referred the question to Rev. Mr. Stone, the Hartford minister who, it will be recollected, accompanied the expedition as chaplain, asking him to pray to God, invoking his guidance and direction for them in deciding upon the course they should pursue. Mr. Stone accordingly spent the whole night in prayer in his cabin on board one of the vessels, and when the morning came he returned to the shore and told Captain Mason that it was strongly impressed upon his mind that the expedition ought to go round by the way of the Narragansett country.

Captain Mason considered this impression upon the minister's mind a sufficient indication of the divine will, and that plan was decided upon.

THE EXPEDITION SETS SAIL

It was on Friday, the twenty-ninth of May, that the little fleet set sail from Saybrook. The expedition reached Narragansett Bay on Saturday evening, too late to land. The next day was Sunday, and they had too much regard for the sacredness of the Sabbath to do anything on that day, so the whole company remained quietly on board their vessels. On Monday there was a gale of wind from the northwest, and it blew so heavily that they could not land. The wind continued all Monday night and all day Tuesday until evening, when it went down, as they say, with the sun. The soldiers then landed, and after forming on the beach they marched immediately to the sachem's residence. The sachem's name was Canonicus.

CANONICUS AND THE NARRAGANSETTS

Captain Mason informed Canonicus that he had been sent on an expedition to invade the Pequot country and punish the people for their crimes, but that all he desired of the Narragansetts was a peaceful passage through their dominions.

Canonicus gave a favorable reply so far as the free passage was concerned, but he attempted to dissuade Captain Mason from proceeding on such an enterprise. The Pequots, he said, were great warriors, and the English were altogether too few to attempt to march through the woods into their country, or to attack them with any hope of success.

The other Narragansetts too, who had opinions to express on the subject, said it was useless for Captain Mason to proceed, for his men, they were sure, would not fight when they came to be brought face to face with such terrible foes.

News from the Massachusetts Division

It will be remembered that Captain Mason's little army was composed only of the soldiers drawn from the colonies in Connecticut, who rendezvoused at Hartford. The quota of troops from the Massachusetts colonies was to come by land across the country from Massachusetts Bay under the command of Captain Patrick. An Indian courier sent forward by Captain Patrick came now into the Narragansett country with news that this division was on the way, and had arrived at the settlement of Roger Williams, at Providence, and would soon join Captain Mason if he would wait for them. Captain Mason, however, determined not to wait. He had already met with many delays, and his men, who were farmers as well as soldiers, and who depended for the sustenance of their families during the coming year on getting home in season to put their seed into the ground before the spring should pass away, were very impatient to proceed.

The Expedition Moves On

So he ordered the fleet to return along the coast toward the Thames, and to enter that river and be ready there to receive him and his party on board when they should have accomplished the object of the expedition, and then commenced his march. A considerable number of the Narragansett Indians joined him. The force consisted now of about eighty whites and sixty Indians. These last were under the command of Uncas. Thirteen whites and a few Indians went back in the vessels.

Fort Nehantic

The party marched that day, as they judged, about eighteen or twenty miles. They were joined during the day by many Indians of the country who followed the expedition rather as spectators, to see what would be done, than in any other capacity. At night the whole troop arrived at a fort, or stronghold, belonging to a small tribe—a dependency in some sense, as it would appear, upon the

Narragansetts—who were called the Nehantics. This fort, like many of the other Indian stations, consisted of a small town surrounded by a kind of stockade wall, which served as a fortification. The Nehantics, either because they were unfriendly to the English, or suspicious of them—or else perhaps because they were afraid of exciting the hostility of the Pequots by harboring their enemies, did not receive the expedition in a very friendly manner. They shut the gates and would not allow any of the company to enter the town.

"Very well," said Captain Mason. "If we may not come in neither shall any of you come out."

So he stationed sentinels and a guard all around the place, and kept the inhabitants closely shut in until the morning. He was afraid, in fact, that if they were allowed free egress some of them might go forward during the night into the Pequot country and give the people warning.

Captain Mason accordingly encamped with his men outside the town, and so many of the natives had by this time joined him from the country that he had been marching through, that it was estimated that there were five hundred Indians gathered that night around the camp fires. These men spent the night in shouting, singing, dancing, making wild and frightful gesticulations, and boasting of their courage and of the desperate feats of strength and valor which they would perform when they met the enemy the following day.

THE MARCH CONTINUED

The next morning the march was resumed. The day was very warm and the way through the woods was so difficult that several of the men, burdened as they were with their arms and accoutrements, fainted from the effects of the heat and the fatigue. After going on about twelve miles they came to a small river called the Paucatuc, where there was a ford.[1] This was a famous fishing place, the Indians said, for the Pequot people, and they pointed out several spots of ground where companies of men had been dressing fish. They concluded from these appearances that the Pequots had been here lately to take fish, and that they were preparing for some great feast

---

[1]See the map of the Pequot country on page 20.

or carousal. Captain Mason was pleased to learn this, for it increased his hope of coming upon the enemy unexpectedly and taking them unawares.

Passing the Pequot Frontier

The river Paucatuc formed the boundary, so that on passing the ford the expedition entered upon the Pequot territory. The Indians who had been so boastful and vainglorious the night before now began to show signs of fear. They became silent and thoughtful, and fell back into the rear of the column. Uncas told Captain Mason, in fact, that he did not suppose these straggling recruits that had joined them on the march would be of any service to them—but that he and his Mohegans would be found faithful and true when the time of trial came. The result accorded exactly with his declarations.

The Halt at Porter's Rocks

The expedition moved on about three miles farther, and then as evening was coming on, and as according to the statements of the Indians they were now within a mile or two of the first Pequot fort, they determined to halt and encamp for the night.

Some rest and refreshment were now absolutely necessary for the men, for they were almost entirely exhausted by the fatigues and privations of their long march. Their supply of food was scanty, as they could have none except what they brought with them. They continued their march, however, for an hour after night came on, though as it happened there was a bright moon to give them light. They crept along as silently as possible to avoid giving any alarm. At length they came to a place where there was a plat of low and level ground between some large and lofty rocks which are known at the present day as Porter's Rocks. The place is in the pleasant town of Groton, and is situated about half a mile north of a small village called the Head of Mystic.[2]

---

[2]For the situation of the Mystic River see map on p. 20.

THE NIGHT IN CAMP

The soldiers took possession of this ground, preserving the utmost silence, and speaking to each other only in whispers. They stationed sentinels in the surrounding woods at a considerable distance from the camp, and those that went off in a southeastern direction, which was toward the place where the fort was situated which they were going to attack, heard the Indians in the fort singing and carousing all night. It seems that from the fort or town—which was situated on a hill—the Pequots had seen the fleet sail by on its way toward the Narragansett country, and so had concluded that the danger of attack from the English had passed, and they were now expressing, in their savage way, the feelings of exultation and triumph which they felt, in finding that their enemy, as they supposed, did not dare to assail them.

ADVANCE OF THE ATTACK

The men slept so soundly, though lying on the ground and with only rocks for their pillows, that daylight was somewhat advanced before any of them awoke. The whole camp was then immediately aroused. It was later than they intended and there was not a moment to be lost, but before moving on, the men were assembled, and a short and hurried prayer was offered to implore the presence and blessing of Almighty God on the work which they were about to perform. Then they set out upon their march, the Indians showing them a path which they said led directly to the fort. As for the Indians themselves, a great many had gone back, and the rest prudently kept in the rear.

Along this path the file of English soldiers crept stealthily, Captain Mason at the head. Not a word was spoken, and every effort was made in walking not to elicit any sound.

After following the path in this way for nearly two miles without seeing any signs of the fort, Captain Mason began to feel uneasy, and to suspect some treachery. He accordingly halted. He sent a messenger back to the rear of the column, with orders given in a whisper, that some of the Indians should come forward to speak to him. Two of them came, Uncas himself and another chieftain named Wequosh. He asked them where the fort was.

"It is almost in sight," said they in reply. "It is on the top of that hill," pointing at the same time to a large rounded hill which appeared at a short distance before them.

THE ATTACK

The force was then immediately put in motion again and began to ascend the hill. Captain Mason was informed that there were two entrances to the fort or town, one on the northeast and one on the southwest side. He accordingly divided his men into two parties, he himself taking command of one, and placing Captain Underhill at the head of the other. Both parties advanced as noiselessly and stealthily as possible, and Captain Mason arrived within a very short distance of the entrance when suddenly a dog barked within and gave the alarm. Immediately afterward loud cries of *Owanux! Owanux!* meaning *Englishmen! Englishmen!* were heard resounding within the fort, and noises arose denoting the utmost excitement and commotion.

The opening in the stockade which formed the entrance to the little town was closed by means of a kind of cheveux-de-frise, formed of stout bushes with the sharpened branches pointing in every direction. Captain Mason and his men made their way past this obstruction partly by climbing over the bushes and partly by pulling them out of the way. On penetrating within the enclosure they found the whole community within in a state of confusion and dismay. Some were hurrying out their bows and arrows and making ready for defending themselves. Others were trying to find some way of escape, or seeking the means of concealing or saving their wives and children. The combat was immediately commenced by the English soldiers shooting down every living being that they could see, and very soon Captain Mason, rushing into one of the wigwams, seized a burning brand and set some of the mats on fire which formed the covering of the huts.

Then ensued a scene of horror which the dreadful records of human passion and hate in the whole history of the world have seldom equaled and probably never surpassed. The flames spread very rapidly and soon the whole town was in a blaze. The English, as long as they could themselves endure the heat and the smoke, remained within the enclosure, shooting down with their muskets every terrified and wretched fugitive which they could see flying from the smoke and flames, and then going outside they took their stations all around and shot at every form which they saw attempting to escape through the doorways, and at every head that appeared at the top of the stockade. They killed many in this way, and the fire destroyed almost all the rest. Seven were taken captive and seven escaped, but of the remainder, consisting of six or seven hundred persons, men, women and children, everyone perished. The whole of this awful massacre was completely accomplished in the space of little more than an hour.

There were seventy wigwams in the town all of which were consumed, together with all the clothing, the utensils, the arms, the supplies of wampum, and other treasures, which comprised by far the most valuable portion of the property possessed by the tribe.

Condition of the English Troops after the Battle

Two Englishmen were killed in the assault upon the town, and twenty were wounded. The rest were so exhausted by their long march, by the want of food and of rest, and by the violence of the exertion and the excitement attendant on the fight, that they sank down panting and almost lifeless upon the ground around the fort when the struggle was ended, and seemed utterly unable to make any farther effort. Some of them fainted entirely away, and were with difficulty revived by the efforts of their companions.

The danger, moreover, was not yet passed, for there was another fort a little farther on, though the force which it contained was, as it happened, now rather small, as about one hundred and fifty of the garrison had come the day before, by the special providence of God, as the English considered it, into the fort which had been assaulted, and had all been destroyed there with the rest of the occupants of the place.

Still the English party expected that those that remained of the other garrison would soon come forward to attack them; and after a very brief period of rest they began to put themselves again in array. From the brow of the hill on which they stood they could survey the mouth of the Thames and the waters of the Sound for some distance around. They looked out anxiously for the appearance of the fleet, which the reader will recollect had been sent back from Narragansett Bay, in order to meet them in the Thames and receive them on board. At length, to their unspeakable satisfaction, they saw the vessels coming into view around a point of land, and entering the harbor with a fair wind. The expedition was immediately arranged in order of march, and began to move forward toward the landing place where the vessels were to await them.

THE WOUNDED MEN

The wounded men being unable to walk had to be carried, and the others were so weak and exhausted that four bearers were necessary to each man, so that two-thirds of all the men that remained unhurt were required to carry the wounded men and the arms and accoutrements belonging to them. This left only forty men free. The column thus arranged began to descend the hill, but before they had proceeded far a troop of Indians from the other fortress, having heard the firing and seen the smoke, came in great haste to learn the cause. On seeing what had been done they were filled with rage and horror. They stamped upon the ground, tore their hair, and filled the air with frightful vociferation. They immediately set off down the bill in pursuit of the aggressors. But the English facing about received them with volleys of musketry and drove them back. They were shot down before they could get near enough to discharge their arrows with any effect. Finding themselves thus helpless they gave over the pursuit. Some went back to the smoking ruins of the fort, others scattered themselves about in the woods, half crazed with excitement and terror. Others still hurried forward to endeavor to find some ambuscade where they could shoot at the passing column of the enemy unobserved.

THE ENGLISH REGAIN THEIR SHIPS

The English, when this skirmish was over, stopped at a brook at the foot of the hill to allow the men to rest and refresh themselves a few minutes. They also made a new arrangement for carrying the wounded, by hiring some of the Indians to perform this duty—Narragansetts or Mohegans probably, who, though they had kept aloof during the fight now hovered about the column on its march, and gathered around them when they halted.

When all was ready the column resumed its march. When they were to pass any swamp or thicket they shot bullets into it before approaching too near, in order to drive out any Indians that might lie concealed in it. Notwithstanding these precautions they were several times shot at from behind rocks and trees, but no one was hit by their arrows.

Whenever any of the Indians thus concealed were shot by any of the English, the Indians that accompanied the march would run off and bring in the heads of the men that fell. The English, moreover, set fire to and burned all the wigwams that came in their way.

They marched on in this way until they reached the river, and there came to a halt on the bank opposite to the place where the vessels were awaiting them.

RETURN TO FORT SAYBROOK

The wounded men, and also a certain number of the others, were put on board the vessels, but as the accommodations were not sufficient for the whole company, including the friendly Indians, and as Captain Mason was unwilling to leave his allies unprovided for, he retained on the shore about twenty of his best men, and took off also from the vessels about forty others—who had been brought by Captain Patrick from Massachusetts, and having arrived at Narragansett Bay after Mason had left, had come round in the vessels to join him in the Thames. With these troops as an escort for the Indians, Mason marched by land along the coast, and in due time both his party and those conveyed by the fleet, arrived in safety at Fort Saybrook, where they were received with unbounded demonstrations of triumph and joy.

END OF THE PEQUOTS

The portion of the tribe that remained, with Sassacus at their head, when the first paroxysms of resentment and rage had subsided, sank into a state of utter despair. The result of the gloomy and distracted consultations which they held was a determination to abandon the country and find their way, if they could, back to their former homes beyond the Hudson. They soon set out on this hopeless undertaking. But the English, utterly merciless in executing what they considered the righteous judgment of Heaven against these Amalekites, were determined that they should not escape. They organized a new military expedition to pursue them. The track which the larger portion of the fugitives followed led along the coast of the Sound toward New Haven and Fairfield. They wished to keep as long as possible near the sea, in order to obtain fish for food, as they had no provisions to take with them, the winter having just passed, and all the supplies of the preceding year being exhausted. The English were, however, soon upon their track, and they harassed them so perpetually on the march as to give them no rest. Many of the Indians perished from hunger and exhaustion. At last the whole body of fugitives were brought to bay in a swamp, where they had taken refuge. This swamp was situated in what is now the town of Fairfield. Here they were surrounded by the English troops, and were hunted out of their hiding places and shot down as if they had been so many tigers. A number of the women and children were saved, it is true, and were given to the Narragansetts and Mohegans, or distributed among the English settlements to be employed as slaves. They proved, however, to be so sullen and intractable that nothing could be done with them.

SASSACUS

The sachem Sassacus, taking with him a number of warriors, made his escape, although some time afterward what they said was his scalp was brought in to one of the colonies in answer to a reward which had been offered for his head. Some remnants of the tribe remained too, and their descendants reappeared often in the history of Connecticut. But the power of the race, as an element of resistance to the progress of English colonization on the American shores, was broken up forever.

CHAPTER IV
WAR WITH KING PHILIP

PHILIP'S FAMILY AND NAME

At the time of the first establishment of the Plymouth colony, and for many years afterward, the most powerful Indian chieftain within the limits of what is now Massachusetts was Massasoit. His home, and the central seat of his power, was in the southern part of the territory between the shores of the Massachusetts and Narragansett bays. He made a treaty of peace and friendship with the English at a very early period, as is related at length in a former volume of this series, and he continued to observe this treaty faithfully as long as he lived. In consequence of the peaceful relations thus maintained with Massasoit, and of the influence which this chieftain exercised over the other tribes, the colonists were enabled to live at peace with all the Indians on their borders for more than forty years.

At length, about the year 1662, the old chieftain, who had been so long and so faithful a friend of the English, died. His oldest son died very soon after him, and the chieftainship, with all its powers and privileges, then devolved upon the second son, who received soon afterward the name and title of King Philip, by which he has ever since been known.

Of course both the name and the title were English, and were conferred upon the successor of their old friend by the colonists. The Indian names which were generally long, and often consisted of several words making together sometimes quite a little sentence, were awkward and inconvenient for the English to use, being difficult and uncertain both in spelling and pronunciation. As the Indians had no spelling, themselves, for their language, and as no system of writing had ever been developed among them, the English were obliged to spell Indian words as nearly as they could according to sound, and of course the spelling of any particular name, as expressed by different English writers, was endlessly varied. The pronunciation of the names was also very uncertain, as some of the words from the sentence which expressed the name were often left out, by way of curtailment. Persons who knew Philip in those days and had occasion to write his Indian name, represented the Indian sound, as it struck their ears, in the following different modes:

> Po-me-ta-com,
> Pu-me-ta-com,
> — me-ta-com-et.

And in other ways.

KING PHILIP MAKES PROFESSIONS OF FRIENDSHIP

The English felt quite anxious and uneasy about Philip when he came into power, having some reason to suspect that he had long been unfriendly to the English, and that he would immediately begin to concert hostile measures against them. He, however, very soon came to Plymouth and appeared before the court there, accompanied by several other chieftains, and formally and solemnly signified his desire to remain on the same terms of friendship with the colonists as had existed in the days of his father. In consequence of this declaration a new treaty of friendship and alliance was formed, which was signed by Philip and another chieftain, his uncle, and witnessed by four or five other sachems who were present on the occasion. All these Indians signed the document by making their mark.

TEN YEARS OF PEACE

This treaty continued in force and was well observed on both sides for about ten years, that is until the year 1671. During this interval a constant and friendly commercial intercourse was kept up between the colonies and the various tribes of Indians who were more or less under Philip's sway. The English bought furs and Indian corn of the natives, and sold them blankets, ornaments, and also unfortunately a number of guns and considerable supplies of gunpowder.

During this period, too, the English, as their settlements extended, made a great many purchases of land. The conveyances of these various parcels of land were made in Philip's name, the English drawing up the deeds and Philip signing them by making his mark. The lands thus conveyed are now included within the limits of the towns of New Bedford, Wrentham, Swansey, and many other places.

Signs of a Gathering Storm

As years rolled on, however, signs and indications of an approaching conflict between the Indians and the English gradually appeared. We have, of course, only the English account of the origin and progress of these difficulties, but an impartial reader at the present day can hardly fail of coming to the conclusion that by their own showing the whites were most in the wrong. Their increasing settlements crowded more and more closely on the Indian grounds. The authorities at Plymouth treated Philip and his brother sachems in a more and more overbearing manner. They summoned them frequently to appear before the general court at Plymouth, to answer for their conduct on frivolous charges. They required of Philip that he should deposit in their hands all the guns that he had, and made him agree to collect and surrender all that there were in the nation. When they got a portion of these arms into their possession they confiscated them, and they made it the ground of loud complaint against Philip that he was so slow in bringing in the remainder.

The difficulties thus occurring led to many negotiations, councils, conventions and treaties, which took place from time to time during a period of three or four years, that is until 1674. The demeanor of the English all the time seems to have been overbearing and aggressive, while Philip, on the other hand, appears to have done everything in his power to conciliate and to satisfy them. The Plymouth government, however, would not be satisfied, and the complaints which they made against Philip in the representations which they forwarded to the Connecticut and Massachusetts Bay colonies, in order to justify the hostile attitude they were assuming were such as these:

FRIVOLOUS COMPLAINTS OF THE PLYMOUTH AUTHORITIES

That "he has neglected to bring in his arms to us as he had promised."

That "he has carried himself insolently and proudly toward us, in refusing to come down to the court when summoned."

That "he has harbored and abetted divers Indians who were vagabonds and enemies of the colony."

That "he went with several of his councilors to Massachusetts Bay to endeavor to insinuate himself into the magistrates and misrepresent matters to them."

That "he has showed great incivility to divers of ours at several times."

These were the principal complaints, and we must in fairness infer from them that in the alienation between the natives and the English which led in the end to such deplorable consequences, the poor savages and their unhappy chieftain were more sinned against than sinning.

GENERAL RELATIONS OF THE INDIAN AND ENGLISH SETTLEMENTS

It must be borne in mind that at the time when these events were transpiring, nearly half a century had elapsed since the first establishment of the English colonies in Massachusetts, and the settlements which the colonists had made were now so far extended into the interior that the Indian and the English villages were a good deal intermingled, and the people of the two races were to a considerable extent quite intimately associated. Many Indians came and lived with the white men, and were employed by them in various ways. The whites, too, had sent out several missionaries and teachers in hopes of converting the natives to Christianity, and teaching them the arts of civilization. Their efforts had been partially successful. Many Indians had been at least nominally converted. The

Indian language had been reduced to writing, and a translation of the Scriptures had been commenced. In prosecuting these labors the missionaries availed themselves as much as they could of the aid of the natives. They selected the most promising of the young men that gathered around them, and taught them to read and write, and then employed them as teachers of Indian schools, and even as preachers of the Gospel.

JOHN SASSAMON

We have specially to do in this narrative with one of these native teachers and preachers named John Sassamon. He lived for a long time with the English and learned the language. He was also taught by the missionaries to read and write, and was employed by them to aid in the translation of the Scriptures. In and near some of the villages the Christian Indians, who were generally known by the name of praying Indians, were regularly assembled on the Sabbath for public worship, and Sassamon was accustomed to conduct the services on such occasions, and to preach to the congregations in the Indian tongue.

It ought to be here remarked, however, that among the Indians who remained with their tribes and adhered more tenaciously to their ancient habits and usages of savage life, there was a great deal of suspicion and jealousy felt toward these half-made converts to civilization and Christianity. They considered them as in some sense renegades from the faith of their fathers, and as liable, in case of any quarrel, to take sides with the foreigners, and against their countrymen.

After a time Sassamon left the English and entered into the service of King Philip as secretary and interpreter, for which offices his knowledge of the English language, and his ability to read and write, well qualified him.

INDIAN INTERPRETERS

The degree of proficiency which these Indian interpreters made in the English language is shown pretty well by the letters written by them in Philip's name, and sent to the colonists, some of which are still extant. Here, for example, is one sent by Philip in answer to a summons which he had received from Plymouth to present himself there before the court. It is very probable that Sassamon himself was the amanuensis employed in producing it.

"King Philip desire to let you understand that he could not come to the Court, for Tom, his interpreter, has a pain in his back that he could not travel so far, and Philip sister is very sik."

Then after one or two sentences on business the letter adds:

"He will come as soon as possible as he can to speak with you, and so I rest, you very loving friend Philip dwelling at mount hope nek."

Mt. Hope

During the time that Sassamon was in Philip's service he resided with him in the Indian stronghold on the shores of Narragansett Bay, which was Philip's chief place of residence, as it had been that of his father Massasoit before him. This place had been generally known during the life of Massasoit, by its Indian name of Pokanoket, though the Narragansetts called it Powams. The English, however, gave it the name of Mt. Hope, by which it afterward was most generally known. Thus the titles of the famous chieftain were two. Among his own people he was called Metacomet of Pokanoket, and by the English, King Philip of Mt. Hope.

Sassamon's Warning

Sassamon continued in Philip's service for some years, and then returned to live with the English again; and under an arrangement then made with them he went to preach to a tribe of Indians called Nemaskets, who lived in and around the town of Middleborough, which is situated, as will be seen by the map, near a large pond called

Assawomset Pond. Sassamon's ministrations among the Nemaskets seem to have been acceptable to them, for in a year or two after he went there, in 1674, the chiefs of the tribe made him a formal grant, by a written deed, signed by their marks, of twenty-seven acres of land for a home lot.

WAR
with
King Philip

While Sassamon was living with these Indians, and performing the duties of a minister of the gospel among them, he became convinced from certain things that came to his knowledge there, that King Philip was organizing a grand conspiracy among all the Indian tribes in that part of the country for a general war upon the colonies.

Sassamon immediately went to Plymouth and confidentially communicated to the governor what he feared. He charged the governor, however, not to reveal in any way the source from which he had received the information.

"If King Philip," said he, "should have the least cause of suspicion against me, of having made such a communication to you, I should certainly be murdered."

THE FATE OF SASSAMON

The governor promised solemnly not to betray his informant, but he could not well avoid communicating what he had learned to the other authorities of the colony, and the story passing from one to another, finally, as is supposed, became known to Philip and his men, and the result proved that poor Sassamon's apprehensions of personal danger were too well founded. These events took place in the winter of 1674–5, and in the spring of that year Sassamon was suddenly missing. Search was made for him by his friends, and at length his hat and his gun were found upon the ice of Assawomset Pond, near a hole. Upon searching into the water his body was found and recovered. At first it was supposed that he might have fallen through the hole by accident, but on examining the body the neck was found to be broken, and there were other marks of violence which convinced the English that he had been murdered. The motive for the murder they could not doubt was revenge on the part of the Indians on account of his having betrayed the secret of their conspiracy.

ARREST OF THE SUPPOSED MURDERERS

The colonists were highly indignant at this deed, and were determined to bring the perpetrators of it to justice. In the course of the following spring three Indians were arrested and charged with the crime. They were brought to trial in Plymouth in June, before a jury composed of twelve Englishmen and four Indians. This arrangement evinced a disposition, on the part of the colonists, at least to pay all proper regard to appearances, in their disposal of the case. The names of the accused were Poggapanosso, Wampapaquan and Matashunnanno. The first of the three, who was supposed to be the principal actor in the murder, was one of Philip's councilors, and was generally known by the name of Tobias, which had been given him by the English. The second, Wampapaquan, was Tobias's son. The indictment under which the men were tried was as follows:

THE INDICTMENT

For that being accused that they did with joynt consent, vpon the 29 January anno 1674 (or 1675 N. S.), att a place Assowamset Pond, wilfully & of sett purpose, & of mallice fore thought, & by force & armes murder John Sassamon an other Indian by laying violent hands on him & striking him, or twisting his necke vntill hee was dead; & to hyde & conceale this theire said murder, att the tyme & place aforesaid did cast his dead body through a hole of the iyce into the said pond.

RESULT OF THE TRIAL

We have no means of knowing what the evidence was against the accused Indians. The result of the trial was that the men were adjudged guilty by the unanimous verdict of the jury—both the English and the Indians concurring in it. The men were soon afterward executed. Two were hung and the third was shot.

We might suppose that the evidence against these men was not very conclusive, since one of the historians of the day relates that the proof which was relied upon in the case of Tobias, was, that the body, having been disinterred for the purpose, and Tobias having been brought into the presence of it, it began to bleed afresh, although several months had elapsed from the time of the murder. It was a prevalent superstition in those days that such a test as this afforded a sure proof of the guilt or innocence of a supposed murderer.

On the other hand it does not appear that Philip, although he was greatly exasperated at the results of this trial, ever claimed that the men were really innocent of the deed. He only complained that the English should dare to execute his friends, one of them an actual officer of his court, on a charge too, which, even if true, did not come at all within their jurisdiction. "What right," he asked indignantly, "had Englishmen to judge Indians for a crime committed against an Indian?"

In a word, whatever may have been Philip's designs before this, he now determined upon war, and he immediately commenced making vigorous preparations for it.

THE OUTBREAK

Both parties held back a little from striking the first blow, each being desirous of throwing the responsibility of actually beginning the conflict upon the other. At length, however, on the 24th of June, 1675, an Englishman, at a place called Swansey, which was a small settlement not far from Mt. Hope, shot at and wounded an Indian, in consequence of high words which arose out of the English having charged the Indians with stealing their cattle. This was the signal for open war. Swansey was at once assaulted and destroyed by the Indians, and the colonies immediately raised a large armed force and marched into the Indian territory.

INCIDENTS OF THE WAR

The war continued for more than a year. A detailed account of the events of it would present to the mind of the reader only a series of sickening scenes of burning villages, of ravaged fields, of cruel massacres perpetrated on both sides against men, women and children, of terrible exposures and sufferings endured by troops bivouacking in woods and swamps, in the depth of winter, without tents or any other shelter, and of wretched groups of fugitive families driven from their homes at midnight by the whoop of their savage enemies, and flying in dismay from a fate worse than death.

Philip contrived to induce many of the neighboring tribes to join him, so that sometimes the warriors which the English had to encounter amounted to quite a large body of men. The principal commander on the English side was Captain Church, an officer who acquired great fame by the courage and energy with which he prosecuted the war.

When the Indians found the English too strong for them in the open field they retreated to some of their places of concealment, which were usually secret recesses in the midst of extensive swamps, containing, however, small tracts of dry ground sufficient for the wigwams necessary to shelter the men. They would fortify these positions by surrounding them with long walls of fallen trees, so compactly laid together, and with the trunks, tops and branches so inextricably interlaced, that a man could not possibly get through without cutting his way. The entrance to the interior in these cases was usually by the trunk of a single tree felled across some deep creek, and so laid that only one man could pass over at a time.

They used also to fortify the wigwams that were built within these lines, so far as to make them bulletproof, by piling up bags and baskets filled with corn inside, thus making the same military provision answer the double purpose of sustenance and defense.

THE FORTUNE OF WAR IS AGAINST THE INDIANS

Although in the course of the summer and fall after hostilities broke out the Indians succeeded in inflicting infinite mischief upon the colonies, by burning towns, devastating plantations, murdering and scalping men, and carrying off multitudes of women and children into captivity, still on the whole the fortune of war was against them. Philip was very soon expelled from his stronghold at Mt. Hope. He was afterward driven from place to place, and so harassed that his supplies were soon exhausted, and the number of his warriors was greatly reduced. His money, that is his wampum, failed too. They say he had a coat or garment of some sort made wholly of strings of these beads, and this, when his other funds were expended, he was obliged to cut up, and pay away the several portions of it to eke out his resources.

THE GREAT SWAMP FIGHT AT SOUTH KINGSTON

When winter came on—that is the winter of 1675–6, Philip gathered together all the forces that remained to him, and went off with them secretly across Narragansett Bay, and thence down toward the coast of Long Island Sound, and established his winter quarters in a swamp near the sea, in what is now South Kingston. Here he fortified himself in the manner already described. He hoped, moreover, that the English would not be able to discover the place of his retreat.

They did discover it, however, and though it was then the dead of winter, and the weather was intensely cold, the English troops marched to the place and a most terrible conflict ensued, the result of which was that the camp was taken, great numbers of the Indians were killed, the rest put to flight, and all the wigwams, together with the stores which they contained, were burnt to ashes.

The English suffered terribly themselves on this expedition on account of the intensity of the cold. The wounded men had to be carried afterward nearly twenty miles through frost and snow, without roads, and without conveniences of transportation of any kind, before they could receive proper attention. But the Indians suffered greater hardships and privations still. Indeed, Philip never recovered from the blow.

THE SUMMER OF 1676

Still he would not yield. He continued the war during the summer of 1676, ravaging the country in every direction, and spreading terror and distress through almost every village and hamlet in the whole colony. His power was, however, all this time gradually melting away. His most able warriors had disappeared. Nearly all his relations had been killed. His wife and son had been taken prisoners, and it is said sold into slavery. His misfortunes, however, far from subduing his proud spirit, only made him more desperate and reckless than ever. His exasperation and resentment seemed to have been made more intense by despair. He killed one of his own best friends for merely suggesting to him the expediency of making peace.

PHILIP IS BETRAYED

The brother of the man whom he thus put to death immediately went to the English and offered to show them the place where Philip was concealed. The English soldiers had long been endeavoring to discover where he was, and a great many attempts to waylay him, or to capture him, had already been made, but all in vain. They sometimes came very near succeeding. Once, for instance, a party of soldiers creeping stealthily through the woods where they expected to encounter Indians, suddenly saw one at a little distance, sitting upon a log. The soldier raised his gun and took aim; but just as he was about to fire he was arrested by another of the party who said, "Stop! do not fire. That is one of our friends."

The Indian hearing the sound took the alarm, and leaped off the log. It was Philip. Another of the party recognized him just as he moved, and immediately fired, but it was too late. Philip leaped down a bank and disappeared in the thickets along the margin of a stream. The soldiers rushed forward in pursuit, but no traces of the fugitive could be discovered.

PHILIP'S LAST HIDING PLACE

The name of the Indian who offered to direct the English to where Philip was concealed, that is, the name which the English had given him, was Alderman. Captain Church immediately organized a party of armed men and put himself under Alderman's guidance. The party were led in this way to a swamp in the neighborhood of Philip's old residence at Mt. Hope. The unhappy chieftain having now few followers left, and probably having little hope that his fallen fortunes could ever be retrieved, had gradually made his way back to the neighborhood of his old home—like a tiger bereaved of its offspring, and hunted almost to death by its foes, coming back exhausted and despairing to spend its last moments of life as near as possible to its desolate lair.

Captain Church, on being conducted to the place, where he arrived very early in the morning, proceeded silently and secretly to set a guard all around it, with muskets loaded and primed, and with orders to shoot down anyone whom they should see attempting to escape.

THE DEATH OF PHILIP

These arrangements having been made, Captain Church put a certain number of men under the charge of one of his officers, and ordered them suddenly to make a rush into the interior of the swamp, and find Philip in his wigwam there and seize him. This attempt was made, but as soon as Philip heard the alarm he leaped from the bed on which he was sleeping and fled.

He succeeded in saving himself from the first onset of his assailants, and endeavored to escape from the swamp. But on the confines of it he encountered one of the guards which had been stationed there to intercept him. The guard, as it happened, consisted of a Plymouth soldier named Caleb Cook, and of the very Indian, Alderman, who had guided the party to the place. Both aimed at the fugitive as they saw him attempt to creep stealthily away. Two rapid shots were heard and Philip fell. Some accounts say it was the gun of the Indian, and some that of the Plymouth man—a double-barreled one—that took effect.

At any rate the unhappy chieftain fell, pierced by two bullet wounds, one of which passed through his heart. He dropped instantaneously, coming down upon his face in the mud and water with his gun under him.

CONTEMPORANEOUS ACCOUNT OF THE TRANSACTION

The accounts which are given of the circumstances of Philip's death vary somewhat in the histories of the day, though they agree substantially in representing the facts as narrated above. It may interest the reader to peruse one of these accounts. It was the story carried to London by the master of a vessel that sailed from Rhode Island soon after the event occurred. It is as follows:

"The swamp in which he was killed was so loose that our men sank to the middle in the mud. By chance, the Indian guide and the Plymouth man being together, the guide espied the Indian, and bids the Plymouth man shoot, whose gun

Death of King Philip.

went not off, only flashed in the pan. With that the Indian looked about and was going to shoot, but the Plymouth man prevented him, and shot the enemy through the body, dead, with a brace of bullets; and approaching the place where he lay, upon search, it appeared to be King Philip, to their no small amazement and great joy. This seasonable prey was soon divided. They cut off his head and hands and conveyed them to Rhode Island, and quartered his body and hung it upon four trees. One Indian more of King Philip's company they then killed, and some of the rest they wounded. But the swamp being so thick and miry they made their escape."

Trophies of the Fight

The news of Philip's death was immediately communicated to Captain Church, who was encamped not far off. He at once repaired to the spot, and having ordered the body to be dragged out of the mire and laid upon the dry ground, he proceeded to have it dismembered and mutilated, as stated in the above account, in the most barbarous manner. One of the hands, which, as it happened, was very much scarred and deformed by an old wound, was given to Alderman, who took it to Boston and to other places, and exhibited it for a show to people who would pay for the privilege of seeing it.

Caleb Cook secured the gun with which the fatal shots were fired, and preserved it as a memento of the fight. The lock of this gun is now deposited in the library of the Massachusetts Historical Society. The stock and barrel, it is said, still remain in the hands of Cook's descendants.

Dreadful Character of the War

The war was substantially ended with the death of Philip, but it was a dreadful calamity to the white men, and very destructive to all their settlements in Massachusetts, Rhode Island and Connecticut while it endured. It is estimated that thirteen towns were destroyed, six hundred dwelling houses burned, and six or eight hundred English persons killed. No language can describe the scenes of suffering and horror that were enacted during the continuance of this awful conflict.

At the termination of it, however, the Indian power in New England was effectually broken, and though isolated cases of outbreak and massacre continued to occur from time to time for many years, there was never afterward any general or organized attempt on the part of the natives, within the boundaries of New England, to oppose the irresistible progress of the white man's settlements along the river courses and over the hunting grounds of their native land.

CHAPTER V
THE LAKES AND THE MISSISSIPPI

FRENCH SETTLEMENTS IN CANADA

During the time while the English settlements were thus increasing in wealth and population along the Atlantic seaboard, and gradually extending themselves into the interior, a line of French settlements was advancing more rapidly still, so far at least as penetrating into the interior of the country was concerned, on the northern frontier of what now forms the territory of the United States, that is, the frontier extending along the line of the lakes, and thence down the Mississippi.

FACE OF THE COUNTRY ON THE NORTHERN FRONTIER

The region which was thus penetrated by the French by the way of the St. Lawrence and the lakes, was very different from that occupied by the English, both in respect to climate and to the general face of the country. Lying as it did much farther to the north, the climate was colder, and the winters were much more severe. The land was, in general, comparatively level and flat, and was occupied by boundless forests, and intersected everywhere with slowly flowing streams, the descent being generally too little to create rapid currents. Besides these streams the country was half covered with lakes which, large and small, were innumerable. The formation of these lakes was owing in great measure to the general flatness of the country which caused all the depressions in the soil to fill with water, and to remain full, since the fresh supplies brought continually by the rains were more than sufficient to replace that which slowly flowed away through the sluggish outlet streams.

Rapid Advance of the French Settlements

One would have supposed that such a country as this, cold and desolate as it must have been in a state of nature, would have been penetrated with much greater difficulty by white men, and that their advances into it would have been much more slow, than in the warmer, more varied, and in all respects more attractive regions that lay at the southward of it. But the contrary was the fact. The innumerable lakes and ponds, and the deep and sluggish streams which connected them, formed an excellent system of internal navigation for the Indian canoes, and made it possible to make long excursions into the interior and to penetrate far into the forests with very little land transportation, and consequently with but little fatigue. Then the forests were filled with animals, and the long and bitterly cold winters made the fur with which these animals were clothed very fine, and thick, and warm. The whole country, too, was filled with Indians who lived by roaming through the woods in search of game, the flesh of which had furnished food, and the skins, clothing, to them and to their ancestors for centuries. These Indians were ready to entrap, and take, and bring to the French adventurers who came among them, any quantity they might desire of the finest and most valuable furs, in exchange for beads, iron hatchets, guns, gunpowder, and also, I am sorry to say, rum.

In consequence of this state of things it happened that while the English settlers along the Atlantic seaboard were slowly extending into the interior, advancing generally no faster and no farther than they could secure the ground by the establishment of permanent agricultural settlements upon it—the French were pushing on far more rapidly along the St. Lawrence and on the lakes, intent only on getting in where they could find the richest supplies of furs and skins. They built forts, and established factories and trading houses, and around some of these stations towns gradually sprang up; but in the main the country was very partially occupied. It was, however, penetrated and explored in every direction.

FRIENDLY INTERCOURSE WITH THE INDIANS

In making these explorations the French contrived to keep always on very friendly terms with the natives. They succeeded much better, in fact, in this respect than the English did, in their agricultural colonies. This has generally been attributed to the greater versatility of the French character, which made it more easy for the French settlers to accommodate themselves to the Indian modes of life, and national usages. It may be, however, that the different circumstances in the two cases account in some measure for the difference of the result. The English, in establishing their settlements, required substantially the whole of the ground. Just in proportion as they advanced the Indians were necessarily dispossessed and forced to retire. They could not derive any material benefit from intercourse with the natives, and so had no interest in cultivating a friendly intercourse with them. All they desired in respect to such savages was to have them move back out of their way. There could not well be a state of things more likely to lead to heart-burnings and quarrels.

The French, on the other hand, having for their object mainly the trade in furs, could do nothing without the Indians, and they had consequently every possible inducement to cultivate friendly relations with them. They could not themselves entrap the minks and the beavers, but relied solely on the Indian hunters for this work. In their excursions into the interior too, they were entirely dependent on the Indians for means of transportation, being obliged to navigate the intricate waters in Indian canoes, with Indians to guide them, and to paddle them, and to convey their goods and stores across the portages by which they passed from one stream to another. They were, also, in all these excursions obliged to place themselves to a great degree in the hands and at the mercy of the different tribes through whose territories they passed, so that they were compelled, as it were, to do everything in their power to cultivate a good understanding with them.

THE MISSIONS

The ecclesiastical authorities of France, moreover, interested themselves very much in sending out missionaries in company with these early settlers, in hopes of converting the Indians to Christianity. Many of the principal of these missionaries were Franciscans— that is, monks of the order of St. Francis. If we may judge from the hardships, privations and sufferings which these apostles endured, we must suppose that they were honest and sincere in their labors. They evinced a great deal of enterprise and courage in exploring the country, making long voyages along the lakes and rivers, and taking a seeming pleasure in penetrating as far as they could into the interior of the continent, and in gaining access to the remotest and most unapproachable of the savage tribes. Many of them wrote exceedingly interesting accounts of their adventures, and of the modes of life which they led among the Indians.

SAMUEL CHAMPLAIN

A very prominent man among the earliest of the French explorers of this northern country was Samuel Champlain. He brought over a small colony from France in 1608, some years before the settlement of Plymouth by the Pilgrims, and after going up the St. Lawrence some way, he landed, and there he and the men who were with him constructed huts on the bank, to shelter them through the winter. This hamlet of huts became afterward the city of Quebec. He discovered and explored the lake lying between Vermont and New York, which has since been called by his name; and he also extended his explorations into all the surrounding country.

The object, however, which he and his followers had in view being chiefly to buy furs of the Indians, the settlement which they made at Quebec was chiefly a trading station, and it was occupied in so great a measure by adventurers, who were continually coming and going, that for a long time there was very little increase in the fixed population. Twenty years after the first foundation of Quebec the whole population consisted of only about one hundred persons.

PROGRESS OF THE FRENCH SETTLEMENTS
TOWARD THE WEST

Still the work of exploring the country and penetrating into the interior went on. In this work the priests, at first Franciscan monks, and afterward Jesuits, were always in the advance. They made their way with a most courageous and persevering spirit into the very heart of the Indian country, preaching Christianity, and carrying with them crucifixes and pictures of the virgin, which seemed to possess a great charm over the minds of the savages—they doubtless regarding them not as symbols merely, but as direct objects of worship. The missionaries set up chapels too, built like the Indian wigwams, with mats for drapery, and in them imitated as well as they could the imposing and mysterious ritual practiced in the grand cathedrals of their native land.

The French were confined, however, in these advances into the wilderness mainly to the northern shores of the lakes and of the river St. Lawrence; for the Indians on the opposite side of this line were in a state of deadly hostility to each other, and the friendly relations which the French had established with the tribes on the northern side, necessarily made those on the southern side their enemies. Thus though they could push their exploring and missionary expeditions toward the west, without much difficulty, so long as they kept on the northern side of the lakes, all their efforts to penetrate to the southward of this line, into what is now the state of New York, and to establish missionary stations there, failed.

On the northern side of the frontier, however, the settlements went on increasing in numbers and strength, until at length, in 1670, about half a century after the first attempts at colonization were made at Quebec, the whole colony, which was then known by the name of New France, contained a French population of about eight thousand souls.

These settlements were chiefly on the line of the St. Lawrence, between Quebec and Lake Ontario. Quebec was the capitol, and the Count de Frontenac was at this time the governor.

THE FUR TRADE

Although the permanent settlements were thus in the main confined to the banks of the St. Lawrence, the missionary stations, as has already been said, extended far into the interior, along the line of the lakes, and trading expeditions on quite an extended scale penetrated to great distances. One of these expeditions is mentioned which consisted, on its return, of sixty canoes, paddled by Indians, and all heavily laden with furs which the Indians had sold to the traders, and were now helping them to bring home to Quebec.

Reports about the Great River

The missionaries who succeeded in making their way farthest to the west reported from time to time to the traders that the Indians often told them about a very great river lying still beyond, and which flowed to the southward. They called the river by a name which in their language signified the *great river*. The missionaries, in writing the word as it sounded to them, spelled it Mesasippi. They felt, moreover, a strong desire to go to it and explore the country through which it flowed. There was one of the missionaries in particular, Father Marquette as he was called, a very devoted and fearless man, who was now stationed at the Straits of Michilimackinac, or Mackinaw as it is now more commonly called, among a tribe of Indians called the Illinois. Father Marquette sent word by the traders to the governor at Quebec, informing him of what he had heard about the great river, and of his desire to go in search of it.

The Governor Plans an Expedition

After deliberating on the subject the governor at length determined on sending an expedition to see if this great river could be found. He made inquiries for a suitable person to undertake the enterprise, and at length made choice of an energetic and active young man named Joliet, a trader, who had been born and brought up in the country, and had spent a large part of his life in making trading excursions in the forests, so that he was very familiarly acquainted with life in the woods and with the Indian modes of traveling, and he had also acquired a considerable knowledge of some of the Indian languages. Joliet was to proceed to Mackinaw and there Father Marquette was to join him.

SAILING OF THE EXPEDITION

The plan thus arranged was carried into effect. Joliet went to Mackinaw and there the necessary preparations were made. Two birch bark canoes were provided, which, though pretty large, were so light that in case of coming to rapids in a river, or to any place where it would be necessary to pass by land from one piece of water to another, four men could carry them on their shoulders across the portage. These canoes were loaded with provisions, consisting of Indian corn and some dried meats. The company consisted of Joliet, Father Marquette, and five Frenchmen who were employed as boatmen. Some Indian attendants, who were to help paddle the canoes and to act as guides, went with them a part of the way.

The expedition thus organized set off from the station at the Straits of Michilimackinac on the 17th of May, 1673. This was the day celebrated in the Catholic church as commemorative of what they designate as the immaculate conception of the virgin Mary. Father Marquette says, in giving an account of these transactions:

"Above all I put our voyage under the protection of the Blessed Virgin, Immaculate, promising her that if she did us the grace to discover the great river I would give it the name of Conception; and that I would give that name to the first mission which I should establish among those new nations."

FATHER MARQUETTE'S ACCOUNT OF HIS ADVENTURES

Father Marquette wrote a journal during this voyage, which contained a minute and full account of the adventures which the party met with. They had a sort of map of the country which they were going to explore, made by Father Marquette himself from the descriptions and rude drawings which the Indians had given him. On this map were marked all the rivers which came in the way along the course which they were to pursue, and also the names of the different tribes of Indians through whose country they were to pass.

Father Marquette was already acquainted with the country and the Indians for some distance on the way. Indeed, there was a missionary station among some Indians living upon Green Bay, on the western shores of Lake Michigan, which was on the route proposed, and it was to this point that the course of the expedition was first directed.

They had a few miles to go over the waters of Lake Huron, as the place from which they departed was on the northern shore of that lake, near the Strait. They made their paddles ply merrily, Father Marquette says, over this part of the way, and after reaching the Strait and passing through it, they entered the waters of Lake Michigan— then called the lake of the Illinois—and crossing the northern extremity of it, they entered Green Bay.

THE WILD OATS

On the shores of this bay they landed to visit a tribe of Indians called the Wild Oats. The name thus given to the tribe was not intended to denote any particular tendency to thoughtless dissipation on the part of the younger portion of the savages composing it, but only to signify that their food consisted chiefly of a wild sort of grain, which the French called wild oats, but which has since been more generally known by the name of wild rice. It seems the country all around the shores of Green Bay is low and swampy, and it produced in those days immense quantities of this plant, the seeds of which the Indians used to gather in their canoes by paddling about among the patches of it, growing in the water, and then bending the heads over the gunwales of the canoes and knocking the grain off by blows of a stick.

The grain thus gathered was first thoroughly dried, and then the Indians would put it in a bag loosely, and placing the bag in a cavity made in the ground they would trample upon it a long time until the husks or envelopes of the seeds were rubbed off. They then would pour out the whole and separate the grain from the chaff by winnowing it.

DISCOURAGEMENTS

Father Marquette and his party were very hospitably received by the Wild Oats, but when Father Marquette informed them what the

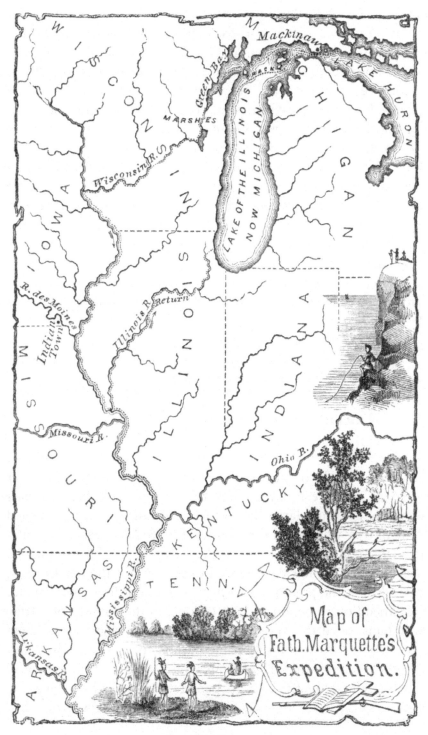

Map of Fath. Marquette's Expedition.

object of the expedition was, namely, to explore the country as far as the Great River, for the purpose as he said, "of discovering distant nations, and instructing them in the mysteries of our holy religion," they seemed very much surprised, and they began very urgently to discourage the undertaking. They said the country was full of warlike nations that never spared strangers coming among them, but would tomahawk the whole party without any warning or provocation; that the Great River, if they ever should reach it, was very dangerous to those who were not well acquainted with it; that their canoes would certainly be engulfed and destroyed; that there were besides great monsters in the river, big enough to swallow the canoes and the men together, and that there was a horrid demon there too, whose roaring could be heard at a great distance, and who seized and devoured all that came into his dominions.

Father Marquette thanked the Wild Oats for their advice, but he said he could not follow it. The salvation of souls was concerned in the work he had undertaken, and for that cause he was willing to incur any dangers, and if necessary, to lay down his life.

So after remaining a short time at the Wild Oats village, in order to rest and refresh the men, the expedition went on.

FARTHER PROGRESS OF THE EXPEDITION

The course which the expedition had determined to pursue in order to reach the Mississippi was to ascend the principal river emptying into Green Bay, as far as to its source, and thence to pass across by land to a large river which the Indians had represented to them they would find there, flowing toward the west and south, and which would take them to the Mississippi. The first named river, which they now commenced to ascend, was the Fox River, as it is called at the present day. After ascending it for some distance the expedition came, on the 7th of June, to the country of a tribe of Indians called the Maskoutens, who lived in wigwams made of mats, which they could roll up and pack in their canoes when they wished to remove their habitations. This was the extreme point to which any missionaries had yet penetrated, and Father Marquette had the satisfaction of witnessing a proof of the success which had attended the labors of his brother priests, in the form of a large cross which was planted in the center of the Indian town, and stood there adorned with several valuable skins, red belts, bows and arrows, and other such things, which the savages had brought as thank-offerings to the Great Manitou, for having had pity on them during the past winter, and sending them plenty of game when they were in great danger of starving.

This Indian town was delightfully situated on an eminence, which commanded a boundless view of plains and prairies, extending in every direction to the horizon, the whole expanse adorned with beautiful groves of trees that were scattered over it, and rich with waving grass and flowers.

CROSSING THE PORTAGE

As soon as the expedition arrived at this place M. Joliet called the sachems together, and explained to them the object and design of the journey he had undertaken. He himself, he said, was sent by the governor to discover new countries, and Father Marquette by Almighty God to illumine them with the light of the gospel. They were aware, they said, of the dangerous character of the work they had undertaken, but they did not fear danger or even death in the prosecution of it. They concluded by asking the sachems to furnish them with two guides to show them the way across the portage to the river flowing west. This the sachems readily consented to do. Accordingly, on the 10th of June, they embarked again, with these two guides joined to the party. A great concourse of Indians assembled on the bank to witness their departure, all wondering to see seven Frenchmen in two canoes daring to penetrate into a country so remote and dangerous, and filled, as they supposed, with such savage and ferocious foes.

The tract of country lying between the two rivers was low and level, filled with swamps and meandering creeks and streams, and so overgrown with aquatic grass and wild rice that it was very difficult to find the channels. The guides, however, knew the way, and finally they came to a landing place where there was a path through the woods to another landing place on the western river. The distance across this portage was about a mile. The provisions and the canoes were all safely transported across this distance and reembarked. The guides who had remained to help in this work left the party when it was accomplished, and returned home leaving our adventurers to find their way down the western river guided by the current alone.

VOYAGE ON THE WISCONSIN

"Before embarking," says Father Marquette in his narrative of the expedition, "we all began together a new devotion to the Blessed Virgin Immaculate, which we practiced every day, addressing her particular prayers to put under her protection both our persons and the success of our voyage. Then after having encouraged one another"—probably by giving three cheers on the bank, or in some such way—"we got into our canoes. The river on which we embarked is called Meskousing"—according to the present orthography, Wisconsin. "It is very broad with a sandy bottom, forming many shallows which render navigation very difficult. It is full of vine-clad islets. On the banks appear fertile lands diversified with wood, prairie and hill. We saw no small game or fish, but deer and moose in considerable numbers."

DISCOVERY OF THE MISSISSIPPI

After going down this river about a hundred and twenty miles, a distance which the two canoes were about a week in accomplishing, the party reached the mouth of it, and to their inexpressible joy saw before them the broad and imposing current of the Great River moving onward with a slow but majestic progress toward its destination, a thousand miles away, in the Gulf of Mexico.

PROGRESS DOWN THE RIVER

They were not satisfied with simply reaching the river, but proceeded at once to launch out upon it and follow it on its course in order to examine the country through which it flowed. They paddled on in their canoes all day, watching everything that appeared along the banks, and often landing to ascend a bluff or hill in order to obtain views of the interior. When evening came on they stopped to build a fire and cook their supper on the shore, and then going out into the stream they anchored the boats for the night in some still water formed by a bay or an eddy, as far as possible from the shore, and there they all lay in the boats to sleep, being in fear of an attack from the Indians if they were to encamp on the land. They saw no Indians, however, for a long time, but Father Marquette, in his narrative, gives a very curious account of the different kinds of fish which they caught from the water, and of the animals they saw upon the land.

Among these last the immense herds of buffaloes which from time to time came into view on the prairies, excited their wonder to the highest degree.

An Indian Village

They went on in this way for about a week, that is until the 25th of June, during which time they had descended the river about one hundred and eighty miles, and thus far without seeing any traces of inhabitants. At length one day in sailing along the shore, they came to a place where there were a great many footsteps on the beach, and a path leading from it through a beautiful prairie. They concluded that this path must lead to some Indian habitations, and they at once determined to explore it.

This extremely hazardous duty was undertaken by M. Joliet and Father Marquette in person. They left the men to take care of the canoes, directing them to station themselves at a little distance from the shore, and to guard with extreme vigilance against a surprise. The two chiefs then set out to follow the path, creeping along carefully and silently in hopes of being able to see the Indians without being seen by them. They had the courage to proceed in this way for six miles, when at length they came in sight of a village on the banks of the river, which here, as it would seem, made a great turn. There were two other villages in view, farther off, on a hill.

M. Joliet and Father Marquette stopped when they saw the village, and after reconnoitering it a few minutes, determined to proceed and announce themselves, thus of course putting themselves entirely at the mercy of the savages, and wholly uncertain what their reception would be. "We first," says Father Marquette, "recommended ourselves to God with all our hearts; and having implored his help, we passed on."

They were still not discovered by the Indians, and they went on until they were near enough to hear the voices of the people in the village before they were seen by them. They thought it best not to go any nearer, without announcing themselves, and so stopped in the path, and both together shouted out aloud.

On hearing this sound the Indians came rushing to the doors of their wigwams, and stood there for a moment gazing upon the strangers in mute astonishment. M. Joliet and Father Marquette in the meanwhile remained where they were, waiting to see what the Indians would do.

Now it happened that these Indians belonged to one of the Illinois tribes, and though they lived far beyond the most remote of the French settlements, they had often heard of the French, and of the profitable trade which the Indians carried on with them wherever they came, and also of the amicable spirit they had always manifested in their dealings with the natives. They were, accordingly, now disposed to receive the strangers in a friendly manner, though inclined at first to act with considerable caution and ceremony. After some delay they seemed to appoint four of their number to come out and meet the strangers. These four, who were men advanced in age and of venerable appearance, came slowly forward. Two of them bore each what the Indians called the *calumet*, or the pipe of peace. These pipes were richly adorned in the Indian fashion, and trimmed with many different kinds of feathers. The men advanced very slowly, and with many pauses and ceremonies, and when they came pretty near, Father Marquette observed that in their dress they wore certain articles of European manufacture, by which he judged that the people had already had some connection of traffic, direct or indirect, with the traders, and that they were probably friends and allies of the tribe which the traders visited. This greatly encouraged him to hope that they would give him and his companions a friendly reception.

FRIENDLY RELATIONS ESTABLISHED WITH THE INDIANS

Father Marquette was not deceived in these expectations. After some parleying, accompanied by many ceremonies, among which were the solemn smoking of the pipes of peace by all the party, M. Joliet and Father Marquette were led to the village and there very hospitably received. We have not space to describe here all the curious incidents that occurred. It is sufficient to say that the Indians seemed greatly rejoiced that the Frenchmen had come among them, and after a time they conducted the strangers some miles into the interior, to the grand sachem's town, great numbers of the people following them as they went, some running on forward, and stationing themselves on the grass by the wayside and so waiting there until they came up to see them go by, and all manifesting the greatest pleasure and joy.

RECEPTION BY THE SACHEM

The sachem was as much pleased as his people had appeared to be with the coming of these guests, and he received them with more smokings of the calumet, and other ceremonies of hospitality according to the Indian fashion. These performances were accompanied with the pronouncing of eloquent speeches on one side and on the other, and the making of presents—those on the Indian side consisting of an elegant calumet and also of a little boy offered as a slave. Then came a grand entertainment, consisting of several courses, in each of which was produced some special Indian dainty. The two strangers were then conducted about the town and shown everything that was curious in it. They spent the night too in the place, sleeping in the sachem's wigwam, and the next morning they were conducted back to their canoes by the sachem himself, and by an escort of six hundred of his people!

The Indians remained on the bank to see the canoes set sail on their way down the river. The sachem, however, first did all in his power to dissuade the party from going any farther, on account of the terrible dangers to which he said they would certainly be exposed;

but they replied that they must proceed, though they promised to call and pay him another visit on their return.

FARTHER PROGRESS OF THE EXPEDITION

It is supposed that the place where the interview with the Indians above described occurred was at the mouth of the river Des Moines, which river, as will be seen by the map, falls into the Mississippi near the northern border of the present state of Missouri. After leaving this place the party in the canoes proceeded down the Mississippi, following the windings of the stream, and meeting with a great variety of adventures, all of which Father Marquette describes fully in his narrative, but which it would carry us too far away from the immediate subject of this volume to repeat. One great object of interest with them in the voyage was to ascertain the ultimate course and outlet of the river. It might, for all they knew when they first commenced the navigation of it, either turn to the eastward and empty into the Atlantic, in the neighborhood of Delaware or the Chesapeake Bay—or continue its course to the southward and empty into the Gulf of Mexico, thus identifying itself with the great river which De Soto had long since discovered in that region; or it might turn to the westward and finally reach the Pacific somewhere on the coast of California.

Father Marquette and his party pursued their voyage until they considered this question as settled. They went down the river more than a thousand miles until they reached the Arkansas River, which joins the Mississippi not more than four or five hundred miles from the Gulf. Father Marquette thought that they were much nearer the Gulf than that, and both he and M. Joliet were extremely desirous of finishing their work by going down to the mouth of the river. But they were afraid that if they should do so they would fall into the hands of the Spaniards, who had before this time taken possession of many portions of the country lying on the shores of the gulf, and so they concluded to return.

RETURN OF THE EXPEDITION

They varied their route considerably on their return, for instead of going up the Mississippi to the Wisconsin they turned in at the Illinois, and passing across a portage there they entered Lake Michigan at the southern extremity of it, and so coasting along the western shore of the lake they finally returned to Father Marquette's home at Mackinaw, in safety, having been absent nearly all summer, during which time they had performed a voyage in their canoes of more than two thousand miles.

FATHER MARQUETTE RECEIVES HIS REWARD

The hardships, exposures and sufferings which Father Marquette endured on this expedition were very severe, and the malaria arising from the swamps and morasses through which, or along the borders of which, he had continually to pass, brought on a disease, which in the end cost him his life. He said, however, on his return from the expedition that he had been amply repaid for all his toil and suffering, for he had certainly secured the salvation of one soul, and that was an abundant reward. The soul which he considered himself as having saved was that of an infant child, which was brought to the bank of the river, when at the point of death, to be baptized by the Father before it died. The occurrence took place on the return voyage up the river. The parents belonged to the tribe to which he had preached salvation through Jesus, on the way. The bringing of the child to him not only pleased Father Marquette very much, as evincing the faith of the parents, but as also making sure of the salvation of the child, through the efficacy of the right of baptism which he performed upon it, at the water's edge, before it ceased to breathe.

CHAPTER VI
KING WILLIAM'S WAR

GROWTH AND EXTENSION OF THE FRENCH SETTLEMENTS

The successful result of Father Marquette's voyage led soon to the fitting out of other expeditions for exploring the country watered by the Mississippi and its branches, and for laying the foundation of new missionary and trading stations throughout that region, until at length, in the course of a few years, the English colonies found themselves hemmed in on the north and west, along the whole line of the lakes and the Mississippi, by colonies of France, and as might be expected, feelings of jealousy and ill-will soon began to spring up between the two communities. The French and the English seem determined to hate each other everywhere and at all times, and the hardships and sufferings which these different representatives of a common civilization endured, and which we might have supposed would have formed a bond of interest and sympathy to link them indissolubly together, in reality seemed to have no such effect. The dividing zone of mutual repulsion and animosity, which has for so many centuries extended along the Straits of Dover and the English Channel, now crossed the Atlantic, and spread itself along the line of the Lakes and of the Mississippi, forming an unbroken wall of aversion and hate, for a distance of two thousand miles.

PERMANENT CONDITION OF HOSTILITY

The hostility which was felt by these two sets of colonists was permanent and continual, though sometimes for long periods suppressed in respect to the outward manifestations of it. It was, indeed, liable at any time to break out in connection with conflicts in which the Indians were engaged, for the tribes to which the French allied themselves were always mortal enemies of those who attached themselves to the English. In general, however, the colonies remained at peace so long as the mother countries in Europe were not at war. But whenever France and England became involved in hostilities in Europe, the colonies of the two countries found themselves very soon involved in the struggle. The first great occasion on which this occurred was the conflict which in the history of the country is called King William's war.

KING WILLIAM'S WAR

King William's War, so called, took place in consequence of the great English Revolution of 1688. This revolution consisted in the deposition by the English people of King James II, and the placing upon the throne in his stead, his daughter Mary, and with her, her husband William, who was also a descendant of the English royal family. King James was inclined to the Catholic faith in religion, and to very exalted ideas of kingly power and prerogative in politics. The object of the English people in removing him was to establish the Protestant religion firmly and finally as the religion of the country, and also greatly to reduce the prerogatives of the sovereign, and increase the power of the people, in the government of the realm.

The French government espoused the cause of James in this quarrel. The king of France gave the exiled king an asylum in his court, and promised soon to restore him to his throne. Of course this at once led to war between the king of France and William, who was now established as king of England. The breaking out of this war in Europe led to hostilities between the French and English colonies in America. The conflict that ensued is accordingly known in history as King William's War.

This William stands numbered in the line of English kings as William the Third, having been preceded on the throne by William the Conqueror and William Rufus. The reign is, however, more usually designated as that of William and Mary, on account of Mary's being associated with her husband in the exercise of sovereignty, she herself being more directly in the line of succession than he.

PLANS OF THE CAMPAIGN ON THE PART
OF THE FRENCH

Although the French colonies were far inferior to the English both in population and resources, they determined at once to assume the aggressive, and they formed their plans very deliberately, even before war was declared. One of the most important of their proposed operations was an attack upon New York.

PROPOSED ATTACK UPON NEW YORK

The governor who had been ruling over Canada for some time before the war, and who had succeeded the Marquis of Frontenac mentioned in the last chapter, had not been prosperous in his administration, and Frontenac was appointed again, just at the period that preparations were making for the war. He was in France at the time, but he made arrangements for having two ships of war sent out from the port of Rochefort, under the command of a captain named De la Caffinière. These vessels were to proceed to New York and take their station off the harbor, and wait there for Frontenac, who was himself first to proceed to Quebec and there organize an armed force to come to New York and join De la Caffinière; and they together were to attack the place. If they succeeded they were to allow all the Catholic portion of the population to remain, but the whole Protestant portion they were to send off to New England or to Pennsylvania, except the civil and military officers, and the men of influence and wealth, who were all to be seized and held as prisoners until they should redeem themselves by paying large sums of ransom money. By this means it was thought that the whole character of the colony would be changed—the Protestant masses being exiled, and the leading men ruined by ransom money and confiscations.

And for the purpose of securing the conquest after it should be made, it was arranged that the houses, within a certain distance of the town, all around, should be destroyed, in order that the conquerors might be better able to defend the place in case the English should attempt to recover it from them.

Failure of the Plan

The scheme, however, thus finely contrived, failed entirely of being carried into effect. The French captain could of course do nothing effectual except to blockade the port until Frontenac should come from Quebec with a military force sufficient to make a landing and take possession of the town. It was understood from the beginning that there might be some uncertainty about this, for Frontenac did not know in what condition he might find his government on arriving at Quebec. He, therefore, had given orders to De la Caffinière to cruise off the mouth of the river from the 1st of November, at which time he was expected to arrive there, until the 10th of December, and then in case Frontenac did not come, he was to go away. Under these instructions De la Caffinière proceeded to New York with his ships, and after waiting until the time had expired, and without any signs having appeared of Frontenac's coming, he was obliged to retire, in order to escape the wintry storms which were then coming on—and so the whole plan was abandoned.

The Expedition against Schenectady

Another of the plans formed by the French at the commencement of this war, was unfortunately more successful. It was an expedition, consisting of about two hundred Canadians and Indians, which was sent down from Montreal in the depth of the following winter, by way of Lake Champlain, to attack the English settlements on or near the Hudson River. The first intention of the party was to attack Albany, then already quite an important town. But the Indian chiefs belonging to the expedition thought that the force was not large enough to make an attempt against so strong a place, and so the party directed their course toward Schenectady, a smaller settlement lying about seventeen miles west of Albany.

It was in the dead of winter that this expedition commenced its march, and the people of Schenectady, not dreaming of the possibility of an armed force making its way for hundreds of miles through the wilderness, at that season of the year, were reposing in perfect security, so that although the town was enclosed by a stockade for defense in case of danger, the people did not even station sentinels at the gates, but left them wholly unguarded.

SURPRISE AND MASSACRE OF THE INHABITANTS

It was about eleven o'clock on the night of the 8th of February that the invading horde arrived before the town. There was a violent snowstorm raging. The fallen snow deadened the soldiers' footsteps, and the raging of the storm was sufficient to drown all other sounds. Still the troops advanced with the greatest caution. The soldiers were commanded to wrap their swords and guns in their cloaks so as completely to muffle them, and not to speak a word as they advanced. These arrangements being made they all crept stealthily forward through the gates into the town.

When the whole troop had entered, and the points of attack had been chosen, they all suddenly sent forth a volley of most vociferous and unearthly yells, and immediately assailed the doors of the houses with axes and beams of wood, and crashing through them sprang upon the occupants as they leaped from their beds in indescribable terror and dismay. Mothers ran shrieking to save their children. Husbands vainly endeavored to protect their wives. Others rushed for arms in hopes of making some defense. But defense was out of the question. The French with their savage allies soon obtained complete possession of the place. Nearly all the able-bodied men were put to the sword. The houses were set on fire, and all but two in the whole village were burned to the ground.

Of these two one was spared because a French officer, who had been wounded in the fray, had been carried into it, and the other because the wife of the owner of it had shown kindness to some French prisoners on a former occasion.

Of the whole population only about sixty persons escaped with their lives. These were almost exclusively old men, women and children. About half of these were taken and held as prisoners. The rest made their escape in the direction toward Albany, flying half-dressed and in confusion, through the woods, with no light to guide their way but the whiteness of the falling snow, though the heavens behind them were lurid with the flames of their burning dwellings.

These wretched fugitives pressed on in their awful flight for hours, all the time breathless with exertion, and bewildered by terror and despair; and so cold was the night that nearly all of them were more or less frozen in their limbs, before they reached a place of shelter.

FINAL RESULT OF THE EXPEDITION

The alarm was of course immediately spread to Albany, and to all the towns and settlements in the colony, and the whole people sprang at once to arms. Of course so small a number as two hundred could not hope to maintain itself against so extended a population when once it was aroused, and nothing was now left for the party of invaders but to make the best of their way back to Montreal.

They accordingly set out at once on their retreat, but their provisions were now in a great measure exhausted, and after suffering incredible privations and hardships, at the commencement of the march, they found they could no longer keep together, but must separate into small parties in hopes of finding more food. They were pursued, too, by the enemies whose resentment they had so cruelly aroused. Many of them were killed, some were taken prisoners. Numbers perished of cold and hunger, and at last only a small and miserable remnant succeeded in making their way back to Montreal.

OTHER EXPEDITIONS

There were two other expeditions sent off at nearly the same time with this one against Schenectady. One was fitted out at Quebec, and the other at Three Rivers, a town intermediate between Quebec and Montreal. The first was directed against the settlements in Maine, at and near the mouth of the Kennebec, and the second against those in New Hampshire. These two expeditions were comparatively small, but they were equally successful with the one already described. After destroying the forts against which they were sent, burning many houses, and massacring many of the inhabitants, they made their way back again through the woods, and over the ice-bound streams and swamps to Canada.

EFFECTS OF THESE EXPEDITIONS ON THE INDIANS

One great object which the French had in view in these expeditions, was the moral effect they were expected to produce on the Indians, and especially on the western tribes. The administration of the governor who had preceded Frontenac, had been so weak and inefficient, that the Indians about the lakes had begun, it seems, to lose their faith in the French, and to turn their thoughts toward allying themselves with the English, who moreover had been promising them, as an additional inducement, new and enlarged facilities for trade. These victories, however, as the Indians regarded them, soon had the effect of turning the scale once more in favor of the French. And in order to complete and confirm this change of sentiment, Frontenac now fitted up, and sent out along the lakes, a very grand trading expedition, with large supplies of goods for traffic, and a great number of curious and valuable presents for the different chiefs. These trading expeditions were carried out on so great a scale that a fleet of more than a hundred canoes was required to bring back the return cargoes of skins and furs purchased with the goods.

The result was that the waning friendship of the Indians was brought back again to its former state, and the plans of the English colonies for winning the savages over to their side were thwarted.

EXCITEMENT IN THE ENGLISH COLONIES

The English colonists were not only greatly exasperated by the barbarous cruelty of the attacks made upon their settlements by their Canadian neighbors, but they felt in no small degree mortified by them, since the population of the Canadas was probably not much more than one-tenth as great as that of the English settlements. It was very humiliating to English pride to be thus assailed and harassed by an enemy over whom they had the advantage in numbers of ten to one. They immediately determined to take measures for putting an effectual and final end to the power of their neighbors to molest them, by invading the country and sweeping the French dominion over it entirely away.

The different colonies appointed deputies who assembled in New York, in May, 1690, and formed themselves into a Congress—the first assembly under that name which was convened in America—and there planned and determined upon the measures to be taken for the effectual extinction of the French power on the continent.

PLANS OF THE CAMPAIGN

To render the accomplishment of this object perfectly secure they resolved to attack Canada both by sea and land. Two thousand men were to be raised at once and marched to Montreal by the way of Lake Champlain. At the same time they despatched messengers to England to propose to the home government to send out ships of war to pass up the river St. Lawrence and attack Quebec.

The plan, however, of obtaining aid from England, failed, for the government of William and Mary was so hard pushed by King James, who had made an incursion into Ireland, and seemed for a time to be going on triumphantly toward recovering his kingdom, that they could not spare any forces to send to America. On receiving these tidings the colonists determined to fit out a naval expedition themselves.

The organization of the two expeditions immediately commenced—and very soon every town and village in all the northern portion of the country resounded with martial excitement and with preparations for war. General Winthrop was placed in command of the land expedition, and Sir William Phipps, a distinguished naval officer, of that which was to proceed by sea.

PRELIMINARY EXPEDITIONS

While the preparations for the grand attack upon Canada were going forward, Sir William Phipps made some preliminary excursions to the northward and eastward, along the coasts now pertaining to Maine and Nova Scotia, in the course of which he captured and destroyed several French forts, and pillaged and burnt many villages. The French and the Indians retaliated upon the English forts and settlements on the New Hampshire coast, and in that vicinity; and these conflicts led to awful scenes of terror and distress for the inhabitants. One of the most terrible of the many dreadful stories related of those times was the cruel fate of Major Waldron.

TREACHERY OF MAJOR WALDRON

Major Waldron was an English officer, now eighty years of age. About thirteen years before this time, at the close of the war with King Philip, when the English were hunting out the Indians with fire and sword in every direction, a troop of soldiers came into New Hampshire with orders to attack and seize the Indians there, with a view of punishing all who had been in any way concerned in aiding and abetting in the Philip war. Major Waldron, who resided there, in the town of Dover, was at that time on good terms with the Indians, and about four hundred of them had met at his dwelling, which was a sort of fort, and some amicable negotiations were going on, the Indians considering Major Waldron as their friend and protector. He had, indeed, assumed that character toward them, but now when the English troops had come, with orders from his superiors at Boston to aid in making prisoners of all these men, he found himself placed in a very difficult situation.

After some hesitation he concluded to cooperate with the English troops in their design. He accordingly devised the following stratagem. He invited the Indians to an entertainment which he proposed for their amusement. It was to consist of a sham fight, in which the Indians were to be on one side and the English soldiers on the other. Care was taken that the Indian guns should be loaded with blank cartridges, and those of the English with bullets. The Indians, trusting implicitly to the faith of an English officer, fell readily into the snare. After some preliminary maneuvers the Indians were induced to fire, and then as soon as their guns were discharged, so that there could no longer be even an explosion of powder from them, the English soldiers rushed upon them, some with swords drawn, and others with guns aimed and ready, so that the poor Indians, before they could recover from their astonishment, were seized, disarmed and bound.

A number of the prisoners thus taken were afterward released on proof being furnished that they had never been guilty of any acts of hostility against the English. But many were put to death, and about two hundred of them were carried off and sold into slavery.

The Indians' Plan for Revenge

Years passed on and Major Waldron supposed that this affair had been forgotten, but instead of that the wound which it had made rankled, it seems, in the savage breast, more and more with the lapse of time. The Indians who were themselves released were filled with indignation and rage at such an act of treachery, and of those who had been sold into slavery many returned, and secretly and silently fed the flames of resentment and revenge, though they dissimulated their designs so well and kept them so secret, that neither Major Waldron himself nor any of his friends suspected any danger.

At length the general disturbance in the state of the country produced by the breaking out of this war, gave the Indians the opportunity they desired to accomplish their end. They, accordingly, matured their plan, which was to gain admission at night into the fort or block house where Major Waldron lived, seize the Major and execute upon him, on the spot, the judgment of their rude law. In order to gain admission to the fort they sent two squaws, in the evening, to pretend to be travelers and to ask permission to sleep during the night before the fire, a request not unfrequently made by Indians in those days, in times of peace. There were two or three other houses in the neighborhood, all fortified like Major Waldron's, and to make their work sure the Indians sent two squaws to each of them. They were all admitted without hesitation. At Major Waldron's house the squaws, when bedtime came, were left in the kitchen before the fire. The people even showed them how to unfasten the door, if they wished to go away early in the morning.[3]

Success of the Plot

At midnight, and at a concerted signal, the squaws silently opened the doors of the several houses, and the Indians that had been waiting in the neighborhood in ambuscade, crept stealthily

---

[3]See p. ii.

in. Then followed the usual scene of consternation and horror attendant on such surprises. The sleeping families were aroused from their slumbers by an explosion of hideous shrieks and yells, and by the bursting into their rooms of bands of ferocious savages, brandishing their tomahawks and thirsting for blood. The resisting and the unresisting were alike slaughtered. Major Waldron, though as we have said was now eighty years old, seized a sword that was hanging by his bed, and succeeded in driving the assailants from his room, and in forcing them back through two or three doors, but as he turned to seize a gun he was felled to the ground by a blow upon his head with a tomahawk.

Indian Ideas of Executing Justice on a Criminal

It was found that the unhappy man was only stunned by the blow which he had received. When his senses returned his captors brought him to the hall, put him in an armchair, and set the chair upon a long table used as a mess table for the family and garrison. Here for a long time they taunted and derided him. Then they ransacked the house for food, compelling the people to aid them in bringing it out, and setting it before them. They continued feasting and carousing over this food for some time, and then they commenced the work of tormenting their prisoner. They began by coming up to him one by one and cutting him across the breast and stomach with their knives, saying as they did so, "That is to cross out *my* account," and "That is to cross out *my* account." When they had satisfied themselves with this, they cut off his nose and ears, and crammed them into his mouth, and finally when spent with loss of blood he fainted and was falling off the table, one of them held the point of his sword under him, to catch him upon it as he fell, and so put an end to his misery.

The Race not Always to the Swift, nor the Battle to the Strong

But to return to the grand preparations for the invasion of Canada. Notwithstanding the celebrated remark of Napoleon that the

God of Battles is generally found ranged on the side of the heaviest battalions, nothing would seem to be more unsafe than predictions in respect to the result of a conflict, based on the relative strength of the combatants at the commencement of it. This truth was strikingly illustrated in this, as it has been several times since, in other invasions of Canada. The English colonists, being in number as we have said ten to one of the French, and the disproportion in respect to means and resources being perhaps greater still, they thought that they had only to put forth one vigorous exertion of their strength, in order to sweep the power of their rivals and enemies from the continent. They were doomed, however, to a total disappointment.

ADVANCE OF THE LAND EXPEDITION

The land expedition under General Winthrop was finally organized, and marched to the northward. The troops advanced till they reached the shores of Lake George, and there they encamped, waiting until they should hear, by means of messengers sent through the woods across the country, that Admiral Phipps had arrived in the St. Lawrence, in order that they might advance to the attack of Montreal at the same time that the ships were assailing Quebec. By thus entering the country at the same time upon opposite sides of it, they hoped to distract the councils of the governor, and compel him to divide his forces. And in this for a time they succeeded.

DISASTROUS TERMINATION OF THE EXPEDITION

The army had not been long at their encampment before suddenly the smallpox broke out among them, and soon began rapidly to spread through the ranks of the army, and among the Indians living in the neighborhood, carrying everywhere the utmost terror and dismay. The art of vaccination was not known in those days, and the breaking out of the smallpox was justly considered as the most awful scourge by which a human community could be visited. In the case of an army, the evil and the consequent terror were frightfully aggravated, especially an army situated as this was, encamped in a wilderness, and surrounded by Indians. In a short time more than three hundred men were stricken down and died, and the rest were so appalled by the danger that all discipline, and almost all organization, were at an end. General Winthrop was obliged to abandon his camp and fall back in confusion to Albany, and here after vainly striving to reorganize his forces, he was obliged to give up the attempt. The men were disbanded and dismissed, and they went off in squads and companies to their several homes.

Relief for the Canadian Governor

This, of course, was a great relief to the Canadian governor, who at once recalled the men whom he had sent to defend Montreal, and now, with all his forces united, prepared to make his stand at Quebec. It was not long before Admiral Phipps appeared with his fleet at the mouth of the St. Lawrence—much earlier, in fact, than the governor had expected him. The governor first heard of his entrance into the river from an Indian scout, who made his way across through the woods from the Bay of Fundy, and thus brought the tidings. The governor immediately pressed forward down the river to Quebec, taking with him all the forces that he could gather by the way.

Situation of Quebec

Quebec is situated at a point on the river where the bank is very high. A. large part of the town is built upon the cliffs above, where also is situated the citadel, a very strong fortress. Below, along the line of the shore, is another portion of the town, called the lower town. It is here, of course, that landings are made, and that the chief business is transacted that is connected with the traffic on the river. A winding and zigzag road ascends the cliff, leading from the lower to the upper town.

The river St. Charles comes into the St. Lawrence at Quebec, immediately below the town, and the wharves and landings extend round the point, and along the margin of the St. Charles, thus forming a waterfront for the town on both rivers. Just below, the united streams widen into a broad and very picturesque bay, which is adorned with beautifully wooded islands, and bordered on every side by bold and commanding shores.

PREPARATIONS FOR DEFENSE

The governor immediately on his arrival adopted energetic measures to complete the defenses of the town. Entrenchments were thrown up along the shore to defend the lower town, and batteries were established at all commanding points for some distance down the river. The upper town was enclosed with palisades, and all the entrances but one were barricaded. The road leading from the upper town to the lower was cut off in three places, and obstructed with *chevaux de frise*—small openings only being left which could be effectually closed at a very brief notice.

THE TOWN SUMMONED TO SURRENDER

It was on the 16th of October that the sentries, from their stations on the cliffs, first obtained a view of the fleet of Admiral Phipps, as it came up the river. The vessels came to anchor a short distance below the town, and immediately afterward a boat came on shore with a herald to summon the place to surrender. The herald, as is often the usage in such cases, was blindfolded, and then conducted by very circuitous and winding ways, first through and among all the different redoubts and batteries of the lower town, and then up the winding road to the upper town, and along the lines of fortifications there, seeing nothing, but hearing the din of martial sounds everywhere. The object of this maneuver was to impress him as strongly as possible with an idea of the extent and magnitude of the works. He was finally conveyed to the citadel, and there being conducted into a great hall the bandage was removed. He found himself in the presence of the governor, who was surrounded by the chief officers of the army, and also by all the principal civil dignitaries of the state whom he had convened to be present at the interview.

As soon as the herald had recovered a little from his surprise he proceeded to deliver his message, which as it would appear was somewhat haughty and overbearing in its character. In fact, Admiral Phipps in approaching Quebec had no idea of the extent of the preparations which had been made to receive him. He had taken great pains to keep the destination of the fleet a secret, and he expected that his appearance before Quebec would take the French by surprise, and would find them wholly unprepared for defense. The herald, therefore, had been ordered to summon the place, in the most preemptory manner, to surrender at once and unconditionally to his majesty King William III—adding, however, graciously, that if that were done, his majesty, like a good Christian, would overlook and forgive all past injuries which his colonies had received from the Canadians.

REPLY TO THE SUMMONS

The governor, as well as the other French officers around him, was quite incensed at the haughty tone thus assumed by the English envoy. He said, that as for King William III, he did not know such a person. He knew the Prince of Orange (this being King William's style and title before he was called to the throne of England), and he knew him to be an unprincipled usurper, who had violated the most sacred rights, both of blood and of religion by making war upon and attempting to dethrone one who was at once his own father-in-law, and also the divinely anointed king and the representative of the true faith, as opposed to heresy and schism. He knew of no king of England but King James.

"Besides," he said, "even if he and the officers around him were disposed to make terms with an enemy in respect to the possession of the town, they would not do it with such a man as Admiral Phipps, for he had shown by his faithlessness and treachery on former occasions that he was not fit to be trusted."

The herald was incensed in his turn at this reply, and he demanded that it should be given to him in writing.

"No," said the governor, "go and tell your master I will give him an answer from the mouth of my cannon. I will teach him better than to send such a summons as this to a man like me."

Having received this reply the herald was dismissed, and conducted back to the landing.

THE FRENCH OPEN FIRE

Immediately after the herald had been sent away the batteries nearest the ships opened fire, and before the vessels could withdraw from the reach of them, it happened that a shot from one of the guns carried away the flag staff of the Admiral's ship, and the flag, together with some of the spars and rigging, fell into the water. Some of the men on the shore immediately swam out to obtain the flag. The men on the decks of the vessels shot at them in the water to prevent their reaching the flag, but they succeeded in bringing it to the shore, and it was preserved a long time afterward as a trophy. It was hung under the vault of the dome of the cathedral, and remained there for more than half a century, until at length the cathedral was destroyed by fire, and the flag perished with the falling of the dome.

THE ATTACK UPON THE TOWN

Admiral Phipps, it seems, was not at all prepared for so determined a resistance as he now found he was likely to encounter. He, however, resolved at once on making a vigorous attack upon the town and the fortifications defending it. After withdrawing his ships beyond the reach of the guns on the shore, he remained two days apparently inactive, but, in fact, diligently occupied all the time in making his preparations.

His plan was to land a force of one or two thousand men below the river St. Charles, with orders to march up along the northeastern bank of the St. Lawrence till they came to the banks of the St. Charles opposite to Quebec, where they would find boats which he was to send up secretly in the night to take them across. This force was provided with artillery and all necessary stores and supplies. After crossing the river the troops were to march up to the heights in the rear of Quebec, and as soon as they reached them they were to make a signal to the fleet. The ships were then to advance to attack the town in front, both by cannonading the fortifications from the guns on the decks, and also by landing a force on the wharves along the shore to assault the lower town, and carry it if possible by storm.

Swimming out for the flag.

FAILURE OF THE PLAN

An awful scene of terror and devastation followed the attempt to carry this plan into effect, but it resulted in the end in total failure. The detachment sent up to the St. Charles was landed, but the troops were almost immediately attacked by the French, who had in some way or other discovered the design; and on their march they became entangled in swamps and morasses, and great numbers of them were killed. The rest found it impossible to get across the river. Admiral Phipps waited a long time in vain for the expected signal from the heights, and then advanced to attack the town from his ships. His fire was, of course, answered by the guns of the citadel, and also by those of the redoubts and batteries along the shore. This scene is said to have been in the highest degree grand and sublime. The magnificent basin of Quebec was covered with ships, all throwing out incessantly from their sides bright flashes of fire, and rolling wreaths of smoke. Other flashes continually appeared from the ramparts that lined every salient point along the shore, and that rose one above another on the face of the cliff to the citadel above, while the perpetual thunder of the explosions echoed and reverberated from the declivities of the mountains around.

The cannonading was continued for two days, and at the end of that time the fortifications were found to be but little injured, while the ships were so much crippled that they were obliged to withdraw.

The detachment sent on shore was equally unfortunate. After spending two or three days in fruitless attempts to cross the river and scale the heights, they were obliged to give up the attempt and to steal back to the ships again in the night, to save the troops from being surrounded and made prisoners.

DISASTERS ATTENDING THE RETURN OF THE FLEET

It was about the middle of October that Phipps arrived with his fleet before Quebec, and now a week more having elapsed in the fruitless attempt to take the town, November was close at hand, so that it was altogether too late for him to remain in the river in the hope of repairing his damages, and making a new attack. Indeed, besides the danger from the impending wintry storms, the river would soon be closed with ice, and the vessels imprisoned. Nothing was to be done, therefore, but to abandon the enterprise altogether. So the fleet sailed down the river and put to sea, but it was already too late for a favorable passage. They encountered a series of terrific storms, and were, moreover, attacked and pursued on the way by French men-of-war that came out to intercept them. The result was that the ships were dispersed, a great many of the men perished of fatigue, privation and exposure, and only an exhausted and miserable remnant succeeded in making their way back to Boston Harbor.

End of the War

It was in the year 1690 that this invasion of Canada took place, and the war between England and France was continued for seven years longer. During all this time the French and English colonies were in a state of continued hostility, and though neither party gained any considerable advantage from the contest, they succeeded in inflicting infinite mischief on each other. The hostilities were carried on in a great measure by the Indian allies on either side, and they were accompanied by the usual barbarities and horrors attendant on savage warfare. French privateers, too, infested the coast and almost destroyed the commerce of Boston and the other English towns, and the privations and sufferings which ensued were felt throughout every English colony.

At length, however, in 1697, the war between the French and the English was brought to an end by the treaty known in history as the Treaty of Ryswick, and the colonies were, consequently, once more at peace.

CHAPTER VII
QUEEN ANNE'S WAR

ENTANGLEMENT OF THE COLONIES IN EUROPEAN POLITICS

All the great wars in which the English colonies were engaged, during the time that the American settlements continued in the colonial condition, were contests waged against the French colonies on their northern frontier, and they all arose, not from quarrels originating here among the colonists themselves, but out of disputes arising in Europe between the two parent nations. The first of these conflicts, as described in the last chapter, had its rise in a struggle for the possession of the throne of England—between the two great religious sections of the Christian world. The next, curiously enough, originated in a struggle between the same parties substantially, for the crown of Spain. The war took place in the reign of Queen Anne, and accordingly in American history it is generally known as Queen Anne's War. The question at issue, however, having been the succession to the crown of Spain, the contest is generally designated in European history as the War of the Spanish Succession. The facts were briefly these:

THE ACCESSION OF QUEEN ANNE

The peace of Ryswick, by which the war described in the last chapter was brought to a close, did not absolutely settle anything except to put an end for a time to actual hostilities between the parties. The partisans of James in England, and his Catholic friends on the continent, were as desirous as ever to restore his family— that is, the Stuart dynasty—to the throne. William and Mary had no children. The next heir in the English royal line was Anne. Anne was a daughter of James. Parliament, it is true, claimed a sort of right to determine which of several heirs, more or less entitled to the throne by the principle of hereditary succession, should be placed upon it—but they did not claim the absolute right of selection at will, as that would have made the monarchy an elective instead of an hereditary one. Both parties accordingly looked with great interest upon Anne. The Catholic partisans of James hoped she would become a Catholic, and that her accession would restore them to power. The Protestants, on the other hand, including most of the people of England, hoped that she would espouse the Protestant cause, and thus relieve them from the necessity of setting her aside, as they were extremely unwilling to interfere with the regular hereditary right, except in a case of extreme urgency.

In the end Anne did pronounce in favor of the Protestant cause, and so was allowed peaceably to assume the crown.

THE SPANISH SUCCESSION

Notwithstanding the hatred and ill-will which still rankled in the hearts of those who had been active in this contest, a nominal peace might, perhaps, have continued for some time, had it not been for a great question which suddenly arose, called the question of the Spanish succession. The king of Spain died leaving no children. The prince, who claimed to be his next heir, and so entitled to succeed him, was an Austrian prince named Charles. But the king left a will bequeathing his throne to a grandson of Louis XIV, of France. There immediately arose a contest between the French and the Germans, each nation taking sides in favor of its own claimant. The government of Queen Anne joined the Germans, in favor of Charles, and thus France and England were once more at war. The war raged for many years, and produced a vast amount of devastation and misery in Europe, and it also very soon extended to this country. The two sets of colonies on this side of the Atlantic, though they had no interest whatever in the subject of dispute, were soon engaged in planning expeditions against each other, and inciting merciless Indians to aid them in carrying fire and sword into the settlements on either side of the common frontier.

OFFERED TRUCE

It seems that the French colony, either from a sense of their comparative weakness, or else from being of a more peaceable disposition than their English neighbors, offered to make a truce with them, so as to prevent the hostilities which the parent countries were waging against each other in Europe from extending to this continent at all; but the government of Massachusetts, to whom the proposal was addressed, would not accede to it. The desire of the English colonists to conquer Canada, and to put an end finally and forever to French sway in this country, had not been at all diminished by the failure of the effort made twenty years before, as described in the last chapter; and now that a new war had broken out in Europe between France and England, they saw that an opportunity was offered them of making a new attempt to accomplish their design. So they refuse the offered truce, and began to form plans for a new invasion of Canada. At the same time they sent a commissioner to England to represent the case there, and to endeavor to induce the government to send out forces, naval and military, to aid them.

THE DEERFIELD EXPEDITION

The Canadians did not wait to be attacked. They immediately began to organize expeditions, consisting in great measure of Indians, for making inroads into the English territories. The first of these expeditions was directed against Deerfield, then the most northerly of the English settlements on the Connecticut River. The town being thus upon the very frontier was defended by a very stout palisade of posts, set close together, and eight or ten feet high. This palisade entirely surrounded the place, enclosing a space of about twenty acres. Many of the houses within were also protected by special enclosures made of logs. It was customary, too, every night to station sentinels at the gates, who watched there until the morning began to appear, when they retired to their homes.

It was in the winter of 1703–4 that the Canadians came to attack the town. The expedition kept their design a profound secret. The commander of the band was Major Hertel De Rouville. He had under him two hundred Canadians and about one hundred and fifty Indians. These Indians were what were called Christian Indians, being professed converts to the Catholic faith, and besides being allured to the undertaking by their natural love of war, and their desire to gratify their savage propensities of rage and cruelty, they were led to believe that the work in which they were about to engage, being the extermination of heretics, was particularly meritorious in the sight of heaven.

The expedition set off from Montreal, and commenced its toilsome march through the woods in the depth of winter. The ground was covered deep with snow, and the men were obliged to travel the great part of the way on snowshoes. Such a march is, however, not so laborious and painful as it might seem, as the snow always lies smooth and level in the woods, and the trees afford a complete protection from the wind, which is always the chief source of suffering and danger in all cases of exposure to cold. The swamps and streams are moreover all frozen over at such a season; all obstructions and impediments are covered, all soft ground becomes hard, all rough ground smooth, and men walk upon the smooth surface of the snow, four or five feet above the ordinary level, completely protected from everything but still, dry cold, the effects of which abundant exercise by day, and blazing fires at night, render almost imperceptible. The winter is in fact the true season for a march through such a country.

THE MASSACRE

The band arrived in the vicinity of Deerfield at the end of February. They halted in a forest on high ground, about two miles north of the town. There they concealed themselves, taking care to make no noise, nor to allow any fires to be built, and waited for the morning. At daybreak they came down into the valley of the Connecticut, and crossing the river advanced over the wide interval land which here borders the stream, creeping stealthily on, in single file, along the margin of every copse of trees or clump of bushes which could help to conceal them. The snow was four feet deep, but the surface had been softened by the sun by day, and then frozen again at night, as usual on open ground at this season of the year, so that they could walk upon it without any difficulty or danger, and they had accordingly left their snowshoes at their encampment.

In the meantime the sentinels having kept watch at the gates all night, had left their posts as soon as the dawn began to appear, and thus when the band arrived the town was wholly unguarded. The gates were shut and fastened it is true, but the snow had been banked up against the palisade so high that the men had nothing to do but to creep stealthily up the slope, step over the top, and descend on the other side. In this manner the whole troop gained admission within the town, and there stood marshaled in the silent and solitary street, awaiting their leader's command, without a single one of the inhabitants having been disturbed from his slumbers.

This pause, however, continued but for a moment. It was succeeded by the sudden bursting forth of the Indian yell, and by the irruption of the murderous assailants, civilized and savage, into the dwellings. The usual scene of terror and carnage ensued. The people were dragged from their beds, and many of them were immediately murdered. Others were bound and laid aside helpless. All who attempted to make any resistance were cut down or tomahawked without mercy. In the course of an hour, more than a hundred prisoners were secured, and nearly fifty were killed. Some, however, escaped, and sought shelter and concealment in the woods about the town.

As soon as De Renville found that his work was accomplished, he assembled his prisoners and marched them out of the place, and then set all the buildings on fire, after giving his men permission to plunder the houses of everything valuable that they could carry away.

It was after daybreak when the attack commenced, and by the time that the sun was an hour high the expedition had commenced their march back toward Canada, taking their plunder and their prisoners with them.

SEQUEL OF THE STORY

As soon as the enemy had retired, the fugitives that had escaped to the woods returned, and they fortunately succeeded in extinguishing the flames in one of the houses—the last one that had been set on

113

fire—and thus provided themselves with a temporary shelter. The poor prisoners were marched to Canada. They suffered indescribable hardships and privations by the way. Among the number of these sufferers were the Rev. Mr. Williams, the minister of the place, and his family. His wife became exhausted on the way, being in a delicate state of health, and the Indian to whose care she had been entrusted killed her with his tomahawk to relieve himself of the burden.

The Massachusetts colony afterward made a great effort to ransom these captives, and they sent a vessel to Quebec to bring them home. In this way Mr. Williams himself and fifty-seven others were recovered; but, strange as it may seem, twenty-eight of the captives had become so far reconciled to their enemies that they preferred to remain among the French and Indians in Canada. Many of them even adopted the habits and modes of life of the Indians, and so gradually sank into a savage state.

The most remarkable circumstance in the whole affair was that one of the children of Mr. Williams, a daughter named Eunice, who was about ten years old when she was taken, was among the number of those who thus joined the Indians. She married a young chief, and during all the remainder of her life lived with him in the woods. In after days, when peace was restored, she often visited her friends and relatives on the Connecticut River, but no persuasions or entreaties could induce her to return to her kindred and people.

Mr. Williams himself and all the other members of his family were ransomed and brought home.

ATTACK UPON HAVERHILL

Another somewhat similar undertaking was directed against Haverhill, in 1708, under the command of the same Hertel De Rouville. The original design of this expedition was to attack Portsmouth, but finding his force not sufficient to make the result sure, Portsmouth being strong and well-defended, De Rouville determined upon marching on Haverhill instead. Haverhill is situated on the Merrimac River, at some distance in the interior from Portsmouth. It was then a frontier town, and had suffered terribly before from assaults by the Indians.

It was in the month of August that De Rouville's troops approached the town on the present occasion. He had with him about two hundred and fifty men. He managed the affair very much as if it were purely a religious enterprise undertaken solely for the promotion of the glory of God, and for the extermination of the enemies of the Church.

Accordingly on the morning of the day when the assault was to be made, he assembled his men on the borders of the forest where they had encamped during the night, and made an address to them, in which he exhorted them to forgive one another their mutual injuries and wrongs, and to settle all their dissensions and disputes in a spirit of Christian reconciliation. He then made them all kneel down, and together commit themselves and the enterprise in which they were about to engage, to the special protection of heaven.

THE ASSAULT

The people of Haverhill were aware of De Rouville's approach, and had prepared themselves, as well as they could, to defend the town. The Canadians, however, advanced to the assault, and after a long and vigorous combat they were completely successful. The usual scenes which resulted from these awful irruptions of savages into the villages of civilized and Christian people ensued. Gates and doors were broken open, men, women, and children were mercilessly massacred, the houses were plundered and set on fire, and the whole village was soon reduced to a heap of smoking ruins.

NARROW ESCAPES

There were, however, some narrow escapes. In one family there was a slave woman named Hagar. She contrived to seize two of the children and carry them into the cellar, where she hid them by putting them under two tubs that were standing there, bottom upwards. She then went herself and hid behind a pork barrel. The Indians came into the cellar and searched it to find whatever would be of value for them to carry away. One of them stepped up upon one of the tubs, to reach something high, but the child under it did not stir. Another took some pork out of the barrel behind which poor Hagar was crouched down, in a dark corner; but he did not see her. Then after drinking milk from some pans that sat there, and dashing the pans upon the pavement of the cellar floor, they went away.

In another case an infant child escaped with its life in a manner which was still more remarkable. It was the child of parents named Hartshorne. The father was shot in the street, with his two sons, at the commencement of the conflict. The house, it seems, was of one story, with a rude chamber in the attic. The entrance to the cellar was by means of a trap-door in the floor, and a step-ladder going down. Mrs. Hartshorne determined on hiding in the cellar; but she did not dare to take the infant down with the other children, fearing that it might cry, and thus reveal the secret of the hiding-place. So she had the heroic resolution to leave this, her darling, in the bed upstairs, and the rest of the children she hurried down through the trap-door into the cellar, and concealed them and herself there. The Indians came into the house and ransacked it for plunder, but happily did not observe the trap-door. They, however, went into the garret, and finding the baby there threw it out the window.

Fortunately it did not have far to fall, and it so happened moreover that it came down upon a loose pile of shingles. It was, however, stunned by the blow, and afterward, when the Indians had retired, was found by the mother, and taken up insensible. The child lived, however, and afterward grew to be a very tall and robust man, so that his neighbors and friends used to joke him on his size, saying that the Indians *stunted* him when they threw him out of the window.

A great many other incidents, combining the strange and the curious with the shocking and horrible, are related by the annalists of those days. In one case the dead body of a mother was found in a garden, with a living infant at the breast, vainly endeavoring to draw nourishment from it. In another, when two or three Indians were crowding at a door to get in, and had nearly forced it open, a woman within ran one of them through the body with the spit from the kitchen, and frightened the rest away. But we cannot dwell any longer on these scenes. The Canadian party effected the almost total destruction of the town, and then set off with their prisoners and their plunder on their way back to Canada.

KINDNESS TO A CAPTIVE GIRL

The French historians in relating these scenes say that among the prisoners was a girl, the daughter of one of the principal inhabitants of Haverhill. She soon became so much exhausted with fatigue that she was almost unable to proceed, when one of the soldiers, a Canadian of Quebec, took compassion upon her, and to save her from being massacred by the Indians undertook to carry her upon his back. And he did accordingly so carry her for a large part of the way to Quebec. The name of this soldier was Dupuy.

ACADIA

Besides these attacks of the Canadians and Indians upon the frontier settlements in the interior, a desultory but terribly cruel war was waged at the same time, for several years, on the northeastern sea coast. Various expeditions were fitted out from Boston to attack the French settlements in Nova Scotia, then called Acadia, and along the shores of the Bay of Fundy. Here forts were taken and villages pillaged and destroyed, and multitudes of the inhabitants were massacred. One of the chief objects of these attacks was the place called then Port Royal, which was situated on the western side of the peninsula of Nova Scotia, on the shore of the Bay of Fundy. After a time this place was taken by the English, and the name of it was changed to Annapolis, in honor of Queen Anne, the English reigning sovereign, and by this name it has since been known.

PREPARATIONS FOR A NEW INVASION OF CANADA

These conflicts, however, on the part of the English colonists were considered as only preliminary to the grand enterprise to be undertaken, which was the invasion of Canada by two powerful expeditions, directed against the two great cities of Quebec and Montreal. The naval portion of this force, namely, that which was to advance against Quebec, must necessarily come from England, but the troops which were to advance across the country by land were to be furnished by the colonists themselves. The distance from

England, and the embarrassed condition of the English government at that time, produced by the varying fortunes of the war in Europe, occasioned great delays. At length, however, the expedition in both its branches was ready.

THE NAVAL FORCE

It was in the latter part of June, 1711, that the naval portion of the expedition arrived in Boston. It consisted of fifteen ships of war, and no less than forty transports, the latter having on board five regiments of veteran troops. The fleet was commanded by an officer named Sir Hovenden Walker, and the troops on board by a certain General Hill.

In addition to these soldiers brought from Europe, a large number of recruits from Massachusetts joined the expedition, thus making up a force of about seven thousand men. This expedition was destined to ascend the St. Lawrence and attack Quebec.

THE LAND FORCE

Besides this attack upon Quebec by way of the sea, a considerable army was collected at Albany, to march across the country and attack Montreal. These troops were chiefly from Connecticut, New York, and New Jersey. The people of Pennsylvania being generally of the Society of Friends, held conscientious scruples against war, and could not take any open part. They could not even contribute money openly and ostensibly for the purpose of carrying on hostilities, but they raised a sum equal to about ten thousand dollars, which amount they paid over to the government, under the name of a *present to Queen Anne!*

The land force thus assembled at Albany consisted of some thousands—the French say over four thousand—and it was soon joined by eight hundred Indian warriors, assembled from tribes in affiance with the English.

DEPARTURE OF THE EXPEDITION

The organization of expeditions of this kind is always attended by a thousand vexatious difficulties and delays, and gives rise to a vast amount of impatience and discontent. This was strikingly true in the present instance. The ships lay more than a month in Boston Harbor before everything was ready. There were loud and angry complaints at this delay, still not a doubt of the final success of the enterprise was for a moment entertained.

The colonies were exultant to find such a force at last at their disposal, a force which they considered amply sufficient to make the conquest of the whole of Canada abundantly secure. The government in England felt the same confidence in the result. One of the ministers is said to have written to one of his colleagues, when he heard of the arrival of the fleet in Boston, saying, "You may now rest perfectly assured that from the present moment we are masters of the whole of North America."

At length the fleet was ready, and on the 30th day of July it sailed. Including vessels of war and transports, it formed a fleet of nearly ninety vessels.

At the same time that the fleet set sail, the land force advanced from Albany by the way of Lake Champlain, and after proceeding as far as to Lake St. Sacrament it halted, to wait for news of the arrival of the fleet in the St. Lawrence, as the naval attack upon Quebec and the land attack upon Montreal were to be made at the same time.

PREPARATIONS MADE IN CANADA

In the meantime the news of the expected invasion produced the greatest possible alarm and excitement throughout all the settlements in Canada. The people everywhere volunteered to join the army. Even the women imbibed some portion of the martial spirit that prevailed. The Indians of the surrounding tribes were invited to meet at Montreal and organize an auxiliary force. The governor went to Montreal to meet them, and there gave them a great feast. About eight hundred savages were present on this occasion, and they celebrated the inauguration of the war by martial games, war dances,

119

and other such ceremonies as are resorted to by savages to stimulate and increase their hatred and rage against their enemies.

After having made the necessary arrangements at Montreal, the governor returned to Quebec, where a strong garrison had been posted, and long lines of batteries had been constructed on the crest of the heights above, and along the banks of the river below, and watchmen were stationed on commanding points at some distance down the river, to look out for the approach of the enemy. At length, toward the latter part of August, a messenger came up in great haste from one of these stations, bringing the intelligence that a fleet of nearly one hundred vessels had appeared in sight, and were coming up under full sail toward the town.

CONFIDENCE OF THE ENGLISH COMMANDER

The French historians relate that so confident was Admiral Walker in the overwhelming superiority of the force which he had under his command, that he did not anticipate any resistance on the part of the Canadians. Quebec would be surrendered at once, so soon as the city should receive his summons, and as he advanced up the river his mind was occupied in forming plans and making arrangements for the security and preservation of his vessels during the winter, on account of the ice, and in arranging his ideas in respect to the government of the conquered country.

He had, in fact, on board his transports, many families that had come out from Scotland to settle in the New England colony that he was about to inaugurate.

DISASTER

These plans were, however, destined not to be realized. Just before the fleet reached the neighborhood of Quebec, and while they were in a portion of the river which was very wide—sufficiently so, in fact, to form quite an extensive bay—and where the navigation was encumbered with sunken reefs and rocky islands, there came up one night a violent storm of wind and rain, accompanied as frequently happens in that latitude, by a fog so dense that the shores could not be seen. Still the admiral felt no particular anxiety. He remained in his cabin studying his plans, and was sitting quietly there, when suddenly the officer of the deck came down in a state of great alarm, and informed him that there was a line of breakers in sight to leeward, that is, in the direction toward which the wind was driving the ship. The admiral replied that it could not be so. It was the officer's imagination.

So the officer went on deck again, but in a few minutes he returned, and asked the Admiral to come up and see for himself. The Admiral did so, and to his utter consternation he found the water all around him white with foam, and saw the crests of ragged rocks lifting themselves up everywhere from among the waves. The deck of the ship was crowded with people all in a state of wild confusion and dismay.

Every effort was made to change the direction of the vessels, and save them from the impending danger. But in spite of every exertion, eight of the transports struck and went at once to pieces, carrying down with them nearly a thousand men.

TOTAL FAILURE OF THE EXPEDITION

This disaster, and the results which followed from it, were fatal to the expedition. The night was spent in confusion and terror, and in almost fruitless efforts to save a portion of the men that were on board the wrecked vessels. Besides the vessels that were lost many others were greatly crippled, and on re-assembling the fleet and ascertaining the amount of damage the next day, it was at once decided that the whole enterprise must be abandoned.

The admiral accordingly soon turned his course down the river again, and on reaching the mouth of it the fleet was divided. The colonial portion sailed for Boston, while the admiral himself, with the English portion, returned across the Atlantic, and after meeting with many disasters on the way, a miserable remnant of the expedition at length arrived in England.

END OF THE WAR

It was in 1711 that these occurrences took place. Some other projects were started for an invasion of Canada during the two years that followed, but nothing came of them, and at length, in 1713, peace was made between France and England, by the treaty known in history as the Treaty of Utrecht, and, of course, all hostilities between the French and English colonies at once ceased.

CHAPTER VIII
GEORGE WASHINGTON

THIRD FRENCH WAR

The third of the great wars which were waged between the French and the English in America was called King George's War, from King George the First, during whose reign it took place. This war was commenced in 1744, and continued for four years. It was marked only by abortive and fruitless expeditions, on one side and on the other. None of these expeditions led to any results, except that the English took Louisbourg, a strong place in Nova Scotia; but inasmuch as the town was restored to the French when peace was made, it may be said that the contest led to absolutely no change in the relative condition of the parties to it, and the limits to which we are confined in this volume compel us to pass it by with this brief notice.

THE FINAL STRUGGLE

The peace which followed King George's War was, like all those which had preceded it, only a truce, and at length, after a very brief interval, a new conflict arose, which was destined to end in the total overthrow of the French power in Canada. This was, therefore, the great and final French war on this continent. It endured for seven years, and is known in European history as the Seven Years' War. In this country it has been generally designated as the war with the French and Indians, being the greatest of the wars of that character. In later times it is often called the Old French war—the term old being intended to distinguish it from the war of the Revolution, which was more recent. Thus many now living can remember hearing their grandfathers, in narrating the warlike scenes they witnessed in their youth, speak sometimes of the revolutionary war, and sometimes of the Old French War, as the two great periods of conflict over which their memory extended.

WASHINGTON

The Old French war is still farther memorable in the minds of the people of the country as having been the occasion of bringing George Washington first forward into notice as a military man. George Washington was a young Virginian—not more than twenty years of age—when the difficulties which led to the war first broke out. He had already acquired, young as he was, a high reputation for prudence and efficiency, and he was employed by the Virginia government from the very beginning, in the transactions which were connected with the breaking out of the war. The manner in which he performed his part in these transactions gained for him a great name, and made him one of the most prominent young men of the country, and thus prepared the way for his being brought forward to take the very conspicuous part that he did in the war of the revolution.

ORIGIN OF THE QUARREL

The quarrel originated in the same cause which had produced the previous contests, namely, conflicting claims for the possession of the territory toward the west, as the settlements and trading expeditions of the respective parties penetrated into the interior, along the line of the lakes and of the St. Lawrence. The particular tract in dispute in this case was the large and fertile country lying beyond the western slope of the Alleghenies, forming now parts of the states of Virginia, Pennsylvania, and Ohio, and extending along the banks of the Ohio River. The French claimed that Father Marquette had discovered that country, on his famous expedition down the Mississippi and up the Ohio, and that they were consequently the rightful possessors of the soil on each side of the river, namely, to the lakes on one side, and to the range of mountains which bordered the river valley on the other.

The English, on the other hand, claimed that they had bought the land, from the Alleghenies to the river, of the Indians, who were the original and rightful possessors of it. Of course there was no way of striking a balance between such claims as these by argument. The only resort was consequently an appeal to arms.

Negotiations

Before hostilities actually commenced two or three years were spent in various maneuvers and negotiations. Some Virginians formed a company for settling that part of the country. Among the most prominent of the associates were several of Washington's near relatives. This company obtained a grant of the land from the king of England. In the same manner the French government made grants to Canadians, and both parties sent expeditions into the disputed territory, to explore the country, make treaties with the Indians, and prepare the way for establishing settlements.

Washington Sent on an Embassage

One of the principal of these embassages on the part of the English, was one sent by Governor Dinwiddie of Virginia, in 1753, and was conducted by Washington himself. The object of the expedition was to communicate with the commander of the French forces that had already entered the disputed territory, to remonstrate against their intrusion, and also to negotiate with the Indians in hopes of securing them on the English side. Washington took with him guides, horses, an interpreter or two, and stores of provisions, and at the head of this party he made his way through the forests, across swamps and morasses, and over the plains, following Indian trails through the woods, and sometimes floating down the streams in canoes, until he passed the Ohio and approached to within a few miles of Lake Erie, where there was a French fort. This fort consisted of four houses, arranged so as to form a hollow square, and was defended by lines of palisades, formed of stout trunks of trees set in the ground, and twelve feet high. The tops were picketed, and here and there openings were made for cannon and musketry.

Within the fort was a guard-house, a chapel for the Catholic service, and some other buildings. The huts ordinarily occupied by the soldiers were outside. They were made of logs and covered with bark. There were also stables, a forge, and other things necessary to make up a complete establishment for a small force in the wilderness.

TRANSACTIONS AT THE FORT

Young Washington and his company were received at the fort in a very civil and courteous manner, and after waiting a day or two for the arrival of an officer of higher rank who was to receive the ambassador's communication, several formal and ceremonious interviews were held, during which Washington delivered his letter from the governor of Virginia, explained the claims of the English to the territory, and endeavored to convince the French authorities of the justice of these claims, and of the obligation on the part of the French to withdraw from the country. There was much difficulty in conducting these negotiations, on account of the language. Washington could not speak French, nor could the French officers speak English, and they had no good interpreters. The French made little reply to Washington's arguments, but after a day or two of deliberation and consultation among themselves, they delivered to Washington a sealed letter, addressed to the governor of Virginia, which they said contained their reply to his demands. It was easy to see from their air and manner, and from the general aspect of things in and around the fort, that the reply was not favorable.

THE RETURN OF WASHINGTON'S PARTY

Washington now prepared to set out on his return, but he found a great many difficulties interposed in his way. He had endeavored by every means in his power to conciliate the Indians, but he found continual evidence that their interests and sympathies were altogether on the side of the French, and he was obliged to be incessantly on the watch against treachery. He found it very difficult to procure canoes, and in obtaining other needful facilities he encountered numerous obstacles and long delays. The season was now late too, and the party suffered much from cold, and found their course impeded by frost and snow. The pack horses became wearied out, and Washington was obliged, at length, to give up his saddle horse to help convey provisions, and to travel himself on foot.

DIVISION OF THE PARTY

After toiling on in this manner for many days, the party made such progress that Washington concluded to go forward himself with one company, in order to convey his dispatches as soon as possible to the governor of Virginia. So he put his dispatches, together with a few articles of clothing and some necessary provisions, in a pack which he strapped upon his back, and taking his gun in his hand he set off in company with one attendant—an experienced backwoodsman named Gist—leaving the rest of the party to follow as well as they could with the bulk of the baggage.

RETURN TO VIRGINIA

Washington and his companion encountered many difficulties and dangers during their march. They half lost their way and were obliged to take an Indian to guide them, and after taking him were, for a long time, very suspicious that he was leading them into an ambuscade. He made a great many difficulties, objected to everything that Washington proposed, and finally became very sullen and ill-humored. At last Washington contrived to get rid of him, and after that he and Gist went on alone, guiding their course by the compass.

CROSSING THE ALLEGHENY

When they came to the place where they were to cross the Allegheny River they found it frozen on each side to a considerable distance from the shore, and open in the middle, where a very rapid current was carrying down masses of floating ice in great quantities. There was no way of crossing this water but by means of a raft of logs. Such a raft Washington and his companion proceeded to construct, but in endeavoring to navigate it they became encumbered in the floating ice, and Washington, in trying to extricate the raft by means of a long pole, got thrown off into the water and came very near being drowned. He clung to one of the logs of the raft, however, until with Gist's assistance, he succeeded in mounting on board again. Then they found that the river had become so full of ice that they could not reach either shore. They contrived, however, to make their way to an island toward which they were drifting, down the stream. Here they landed and waited in vain all that day for the river to become clear. They were obliged to spend the night on the island, and they suffered very much from the cold. Gist's hands and feet were actually touched with frost.

The next morning they succeeded in reaching the shore, and soon afterward they made their way to the house of an Indian trader who lived on the frontier, where they were comfortably provided for.

SAFE ARRIVAL AT LAST

After meeting with many other curious adventures which cannot be here particularly detailed, Washington arrived safely at Williamsburg, where the governor resided, and delivered his dispatches. The French letter was found to be very courteous and civil, but evasive in respect to the question at issue. As soon as the purport of it was known the governor at once understood that the French had no intention of giving up the territory in dispute, and only replied courteously and evasively in order to gain time to enable them to complete their preparations for defending it. So the governor immediately began to make preparations for war.

DIFFICULTIES AND DELAYS

The governor, however, encountered a great many difficulties and delays in carrying his plans into effect. There was not a very good understanding between himself and the legislature of Virginia, and they were for a time slow to adopt the measures which he required of them. He was a man of a lofty and aristocratic spirit, and entertained very exalted views of the executive prerogatives of a governor. He considered himself, in fact, as a sort of viceroy in Virginia, while on the other hand, the legislature was strongly tinctured with democratic principles, and the members were somewhat jealous of the authority which the governor was disposed to assume. Then there were long and tedious negotiations to be carried on with the other English colonies, to induce their cooperation in the work of expelling the

French from the disputed territory; and communications also to be sent to England to procure the sanction of the home government to the proposed proceedings, and to obtain aid from the mother country. One or two years were consumed in these and similar proceedings before the time arrived for the commencement of hostilities on any extended scale.

FIRM ATTEMPTS TO TAKE POSSESSION OF THE COUNTRY

In the meantime, however, the governor was not idle in respect to efforts for obtaining the first possession of the territory in question. Several hastily organized expeditions were sent into the country by the French and the English, both eager to be the first to get possession of the ground. In these exploring tours, and in the skirmishes which they led to, Washington took a very active and prominent part. Minute accounts of his various adventures during this period, and of the hardships, toils and privations which he and his men endured, are given in the annals of those days, but we are obliged to pass them all by in this narrative, and proceed at once to the more decisive commencement of hostilities which took place in 1755.

FORT DUQUESNE

It is, however, necessary to premise that among the important points which both the combatants were most eager to obtain first possession of, was that at the confluence of the Monongahela and Allegheny, where these two rivers, by their junction, formed the Ohio—the site at the present day of the city of Pittsburg. The situation of this place gave it great importance. Governor Dinwiddie accordingly, as soon as he found that hostilities were inevitable, sent forward several parties to take and hold it. One party was sent forward at once to take immediate possession of the ground, and commence the construction of a fort. Another followed more slowly, making a road through the woods for the purpose of transporting artillery. A third, bringing the artillery, provisions, and other necessaries, came last.

These plans were all well-formed, and the result would have been very advantageous to the English cause, if the French had allowed the governor time to carry them into full effect. But while the first party were engaged in their preliminary operations at the fort, a very large force, consisting of about a thousand men, with field-pieces and all other necessary munitions of war, the whole transported by means of a fleet of sixty flat-bottomed boats and three hundred canoes, came down the Allegheny River, from the fort of Venango, and surprised them at their work, before they had made any preparations whatever for defending themselves. The result was that the English were compelled at once to abandon the ground, and the French took possession of it. They immediately constructed a spacious and extended fortification, which they named Fort Duquesne, in honor of the governor of Canada. This fort became subsequently for a long time the great center of attack and defense by both parties, in the military operations that ensued.

GENERAL BRADDOCK

At length, in the year 1755, as has already been intimated, the plans formed by the British government in conjunction with the governors of the several colonies, were ready to be put into execution. Arrangements were made for sending four different expeditions to attack the French settlements and strongholds along the frontier, and General Braddock, an officer of very high reputation in military circles in London, was sent out to take the command. Of these expeditions he resolved to undertake personally the one which was destined to attack Fort Duquesne. He came with very exalted ideas of the military superiority of regular English troops, and of the drill and discipline practiced in the Guards, a corps with which he had long been connected in London. Indeed, he quite despised such soldiers as could be made out of farmers' sons and provincial backwoodsmen, and in coming to conduct a military enterprise in the colonies he expected greatly to excite the wonder and admiration of the natives, by showing them how to carry out such operations in true military style.

ARRIVAL OF THE TROOPS

General Braddock and his suite arrived in Virginia in February. He was followed soon after by a squadron of two ships of war and several transports, on board of which were two regiments of five hundred men each, and a train of artillery, with all the necessary supplies and munitions of war.

The vessels sailed up the Potomac to Alexandria, and there the men and stores were landed.

PREPARATIONS FOR THE CAMPAIGN

Of course the arrival and landing of so large a force of European troops at such a town produced a scene of great martial excitement. All was bustle and movement. The men established their encampment near the town. The cannon and stores were landed. In addition to the field-pieces, several guns belonging to the ships were landed, and thirty seamen, under the command of naval officers, were sent to accompany them. The services of these men would be required to rig tackles sometimes, to get the cannon over difficult places, and also to assist in navigating boats and rafts across rivers when it should become necessary to use them. Besides these preparations, contracts had been made for large numbers of horses and wagons, which were to be ready at designated points on the route, to assist in the transportation.

WASHINGTON JOINS THE EXPEDITION

While these preparations were going on, Washington was residing at Mt. Vernon, to which place he had retired at the close of his former campaigns. Mt. Vernon is very near Alexandria, and Washington often rode over to the latter place to witness the progress of the preparations. At length he signified a strong desire to accompany the expedition, and General Braddock, when at length he arrived at Alexandria, from a visit which he had been paying to the governor of Virginia, and heard the high character which the young officer sustained, and learned moreover how well acquainted he was with the country which they were to traverse, offered him an honorary appointment on his staff. This offer Washington at once accepted.

THE FIRST STAGE OF THE MARCH

On the 14th of April a grand council was held, at which four or five governors and lieutenant-governors from the most important colonies, who had come to Alexandria for the purpose, took part. The general plan of the campaign was here decided upon, and a few days afterward the column commenced its march. It was encumbered with a vast amount of baggage, which Washington and the others who were acquainted with the country thought would greatly impede their progress. They warned General Braddock of this danger, but he only smiled and gave them to understand that he knew what he was about.

He himself commenced the march in great state. He rode in a carriage which he had purchased of the governor of Maryland, and which was drawn by dashing horses, and he was attended by a troop of guards, as if he had been on parade in one of the parks of London. The column formed by the army on its march, including the trains of artillery and baggage, occupied a space of four miles. Of course such a body of troops proceeded very slowly, the men being obliged in a great measure to make the road, and to construct many bridges as they advanced. At length after some weeks they arrived at the first halting-place, which was at Fort Cumberland at the mouth of Wills Creek.

Here the army remained some time in camp, waiting for new levies to come in from the surrounding country, and also for horses and wagons, for which this had been the appointed place of rendezvous.

THE CAMP AT FORT CUMBERLAND

During the time that the expedition remained at Fort Cumberland the general kept up great state, and exacted of all under his command the strictest attention to every detail of military ceremonial. The mode of celebrating divine service on Sundays, of conducting funerals in case of any deaths that occurred, and the trial and punishment of offenses, were all regulated with as much formality as would have been required in an encampment in time of peace, in the suburbs of London. The general gave elegant entertainments, too, to the officers, having brought with him two cooks and a full supply of all necessary condiments and sauces. At these entertainments the most punctilious attention was paid to all the ceremony and etiquette of military life.

THE INDIAN AUXILIARIES

While the force remained at Fort Cumberland a body of Indian auxiliaries that had been engaged to accompany the expedition, came in. They were under the command of chiefs, with such whimsical names as Scarooyadi, White Thunder, and Silver Heels. These chiefs brought their squaws with them. The name of one of these squaws, who seems to have been quite a belle among the English officers, was Bright Lightning. The Indian chiefs became soon quite jealous of the fondness which their wives seemed to manifest for the attentions of the English officers, and some very serious quarrels would have ensued had it not been that the squaws were soon all sent home again.

BRADDOCK'S UNPOPULARITY

General Braddock made himself very unpopular among all parties, by his conduct and demeanor while at Fort Cumberland. He was dictatorial, haughty, and overbearing. He made endless complaints against the colonial authorities, for not furnishing him with means of transportation more abundantly, and expressed himself on the subject in such a manner to the provincial officers around him, as to awaken their resentment very strongly. As for the Indian allies, he offended them so much by his inconsiderate and domineering conduct toward them, that before he was ready to resume the march nearly all of them went away.

THE MARCH REBUKED

At length all was ready and the march was resumed. The way led now through a wild and uninhabited country, crossed by ranges of hills and mountains, with deep valleys and rapid streams between. The advance of such an army, encumbered as it was with long trains of wagons and of artillery, was necessarily very slow. It would be very interesting, if our space would allow, to relate in detail the difficulties which were encountered, and the means resorted to for surmounting them, and to describe the various scenes and incidents that occurred on the way. So slow was the progress of the troops that a *month* was consumed in advancing a distance of not much over a hundred miles. At length, however, the expedition arrived at a point on the eastern bank of the Monongahela River, a few miles above Fort Duquesne, and after a short halt the preparations were made for advancing to the attack.

DOUBLE CROSSING OF THE RIVER

It was found here that the army could not proceed down the river on the eastern side on account of the high land on that side coming so near the shore as only to allow a very narrow pass between the steep declivity and the water. But the river could be forded, and on the other side lay a comparatively open and level country. It was determined, therefore, to cross the river and march down on the western side to a point nearly opposite to the fort, and then to recross to the eastern side and advance to the attack.

The preparations were made by General Braddock for effecting these two crossings, in a very formal and regular manner, and with all the pomp and circumstance of war. The time was midsummer, the scenery along the banks of the river was picturesque and charming, and the day was beautiful. The plans for sending forward the advance guard, for stationing outposts, for moving the different columns, and for placing the artillery to protect the line of march, were all admirably arranged, and the whole affair formed, for those who witnessed it, a brilliant and most imposing spectacle. If the object of General Braddock had been only to show to the wondering backwoodsmen what an English officer's idea was of the true military style of crossing a river, his wish would have been completely gratified.

THE ATTACK

Scarcely, however, had the troops fairly reached the eastern bank after the second crossing, and commenced their march toward the fort, when suddenly an irruption of French and Indians was made upon the advance guard, and upon the flanks of the column, with sharp and continued firing from every species of ambuscade, and yells and outcries from the Indians frightful to hear. The English soldiers were panic-stricken. They attempted for a time to stand their ground, but were soon thrown entirely into confusion. The English officers did their duty nobly. They made every possible exertion to rally their men. Braddock himself remained in the thickest of the fight. Five horses were shot under him. At last a bullet passed through his arm and entered his breast. He fell from his horse mortally wounded.

CARNAGE AND ROUT

The carnage among the English officers was dreadful. Out of eighty-six, sixty-two were either killed or wounded. Washington had two horses shot under him, but he himself escaped unhurt. The rout of the army was utter and overwhelming. The men abandoned everything and made their way in squads back across the river, intent only on saving their lives. The enemy were, fortunately, too much occupied in seizing and securing the plunder to follow them.

RETREAT OF THE ARMY

Those who escaped from the battlefield came to a halt and reassembled about a quarter of a mile beyond the river. Here Braddock's wounds were roughly dressed, and he was placed upon a litter. He was still able feebly to give orders. The men were, however, wholly beyond control, and were rapidly withdrawing. Washington was sent back on horseback to the nearest camp to bring up succors and supplies in order to enable the remnant of the army to make good its retreat.

Thus was this grand expedition, which it had consumed more than a year to organize and perfect, which had cost so large a sum of money, and was advancing with so much pomp and parade, to secure, as its leader supposed, an easy and certain victory, overwhelmed, broken up, and totally ruined in a single day.

General Braddock lingered a few days on his litter and then died. They buried him silently in the camp where he died—afraid to make any sound that might attract the attention of the Indians. The remnant of the force that was left made their way back again to Virginia, mainly under the guidance of Washington.

CHAPTER IX
THE CONQUEST OF CANADA

Slow Progress of the War

After the disastrous failure of General Braddock's attempt to gain possession of the valley of the Ohio, the war lingered on for two or three years without any decisive results in favor of either side. The colonists, however, during this period were not idle. Under the direction and with the aid of the home government they fitted out various fresh expeditions, and advanced to attack the French at various points along the frontier. But nothing was accomplished. The history of these attempts, and the strange and curious scenes and incidents which occurred in the prosecution of them, as described in the reports and journals of those times, are full of interest, but we have not space to dwell upon them here. We must pass on at once to the grand and final act of the great drama which the contest between France and England, for the control of this continent, presented to mankind. This final act, by which the struggle was substantially closed, was the conquest of Quebec in 1759, four years after the repulse of General Braddock before Fort Duquesne.

Despondency of the Canadian Government

Although no great and decided success had been achieved on either side during the four years above referred to, both sides had suffered severely, and the Canadians, being originally far the weakest party, were left of course in the greatest state of exhaustion; and during the winter of 1758-9, in looking forward to the campaign of the following summer, both the government and the people were oppressed with great despondency in respect to the prospect before them. So great a number of men had been drawn off from the settlements to supply the armies, nearly all of whom had either been killed in battle or had perished from sickness and exposure, that scarcely any were left to till the ground. The supply of food for the inhabitants had accordingly greatly fallen off, and now the whole colony was threatened with famine. No more men could be raised, and of course, no fresh armies could be put into the field to resist the advance of the English forces. And yet these forces were now pressing hard upon them in various points along the frontier, and were preparing, as soon as spring should open, to attack them with renewed vigor.

THE MARQUIS DE MONTCALM

The commander-in-chief of the French armies in Canada was the Marquis de Montcalm. He was a gallant soldier, who fought long and bravely in a failing cause, and in the end sacrificed his life in his hopeless struggles to maintain it. He had been fighting during the preceding season on the shores of Lake Champlain, along which a powerful English force was advancing toward Montreal. He maintained his ground successfully in many great combats, but still the overpowering superiority of the English enabled them to make good all losses, and to come on, after every defeat, with fresh forces to renew the combat.

Montcalm saw that without great reinforcements from France, and large supplies from that country, all would certainly be lost during the next campaign. He wrote imploring letters to the government at home to send out these reinforcements and supplies. But the government was already involved in great difficulty and embarrassment by the pressure of the war in Europe. Besides this, the English were much more powerful than the French at sea, and the passage across the Atlantic was greatly exposed. The government was apprehensive that if they were to send men or supplies the ships would fall into the hands of the enemy on the way.

They were obliged, therefore, to leave Montcalm mainly to his own resources and to those of the colony, exhausted as they were. Montcalm had no hope in respect to the result. He should, however, stand at his post, he said, as long as he had any strength remaining. His only desire was to find a grave for himself in the ruins of the colony which he could no longer hope to save.

GRAND NAVAL EXPEDITION

In the meantime, during the winter of 1758–9 a grand naval expedition for the conquest of Quebec was fitted out in England. This expedition sailed about the middle of February. The appointed place of rendezvous for the fleet on the American coast was Louisbourg, but on the arrival of the ships on the coast the harbor of Louisbourg was found still blocked up with ice, and so they proceeded to Halifax. When all the vessels had got in it was found that the fleet consisted of more than twenty first class ships of war, and the same number of frigates and smaller armed vessels.

Besides the seamen belonging to these ships, the fleet brought over nine regiments of veteran troops for operations on land. The whole force was under the command of Major General Wolfe.

PREPARATIONS FOR ENTERING THE RIVER

The commander remained with the fleet in Halifax Harbor for a time, recruiting the men after the voyage and repairing damages, and then when the ice had melted away the whole fleet sailed for Louisbourg, that port being nearer the mouth of the river. Here the final preparations were made. At length, about the 1st of June, all was ready, and the orders were given to sail. But so great was the number of vessels of all sorts engaged in this grand enterprise that it took nearly a week for them all to get out of the harbor.

SITUATION OF QUEBEC

The reader must here recall to mind the situation of Quebec as described in a former chapter. The river St. Lawrence forms a long and gradually widening estuary as it joins the gulf. At the head of this estuary is the island of Orleans, which comprises a large tract of fertile land nearly twenty miles long and four or five wide. This island divides the river into two channels, and just above it is the bay or harbor of Quebec. At the head of this bay, four or five miles above the upper end of the island, stands the town. It is situated on the left bank of the river, at a point where the river St. Charles enters the St.

Lawrence, coming from the north and west. The point between these two rivers is formed by a lofty tableland bordered by precipitous cliffs toward the river. The town is built partly upon the tableland above, and partly along the beach below.

ADVANCE OF THE FLEET

The English fleet crossed the Gulf of St. Lawrence and entered the broad estuary which forms the mouth of the river. The French had secretly set all sorts of obstructions in the stream, especially at the points where there was any difficulty or danger in the navigation. The English admiral sent forward a number of vessels as an advanced guard to examine all these places, and remove the obstructions, and thus the fleet ascended the river in safety as far as to the island of Orleans. The command landed the troops upon the island and encamped them there.

THE PROCLAMATION

The first step taken by General Wolfe after establishing his force on the island of Orleans, and securing his ships—which he stationed in detachments at the various anchoring grounds around the harbor, where they could lie least exposed to the enemy's batteries, and could at the same time best command the approaches to the city—was to attempt to draw off the peasant population of the country from their government, by issuing a proclamation. In this proclamation he assured them that he had come to wage war not against them, but against the government alone, and promised them protection if they would remain peaceably at their homes.

The proclamation produced much the same effect that such appeals to the people of an invaded country usually do. The peasantry remained true to their allegiance, and did everything in their power not only to aid General Montcalm in all his endeavors, but also to harass the English troops by every possible means. They watched the camps, and cut off and murdered all stragglers. This led to cruel acts of revenge and retaliation on the part of the English soldiers, and a great deal of suffering was thus occasioned on both sides, by acts of hostility which only aggravated the horrors of the contest, without producing any appreciable effect on the result.

CANNONADING IN THE HARBOR

It was on the 26th of June that the English troops took possession of the island of Orleans, and on the 28th that General Wolfe issued his proclamation. After this nearly two weeks were spent by the English in strengthening and securing their encampment on the island, and in getting possession of various commanding positions on the shores of the harbor and of the neighboring waters, from which they hoped to be able to establish batteries. These attempts were, of course, resisted by the French, and in some cases obstinate and bloody conflicts ensued. There was, in particular, a protracted contest for the possession of a sort of promontory named Point Levi, which was nearly opposite Quebec, though a little below. In the end the English were victorious, and obtained possession of the point, and they immediately erected formidable batteries upon it, from which they cannonaded the city. By this fire they damaged the works on the heights, and they almost entirely destroyed the lower town.

THE FRENCH FIRE-SHIPS

The French made one very formidable attempt to destroy the English fleet by means of fire-ships. They chose the time for this attempt immediately after a violent storm, when they knew the vessels must have been more or less damaged in their rigging and disturbed in their moorings, and when consequently the crews would be necessarily engaged with more or less of hurry and confusion in making repairs. *Seven* fire-ships were prepared, and after being loaded with all sorts of combustibles and set on fire, were delivered to the current at midnight, to be borne down to the anchorage ground of the English fleet.

This project, however, did not succeed, for the English admiral immediately manned his boats with the most resolute and fearless men among the crews, and sent them out to intercept the fire-ships. The crews of these boats contrived to approach near enough to the ships, all in flames as they were, to attach tow-lines to them, and by means of these they towed them away into shoal water, where they got aground, and there burnt to the water's edge without doing any harm.

Reconnoitering Party

In these and similar operations, the last week in June and the first and second weeks in July passed away. The English were gradually gaining ground, it is true, but thus far no decided advantage had been secured. The whole shore on the northern side of the river, for four or five miles below Quebec, was in the hands of the French, and was strongly fortified. The tract extended from the river St. Charles, which enters the St. Lawrence at Quebec, down to the river Montmorency, several miles below. This river flows through a deep ravine, and the left wing of the French army rested on the bank of it, which was high and precipitous. The English had posted a strong force below the mouth of the Montmorency, and now the general determined to send a reconnoitering party up that river, in order to examine the banks of it and find some place for crossing, so as to attack the French in the rear.

The reconnoitering party accordingly marched up the river on the northern and eastern bank, but they found that in every place where there was a possibility of crossing with the troops, the French had made intrenchments and planted batteries to defend the passage, and these were too strong and too well guarded to make it prudent to attempt to force them.

The making of a reconnaissance like this, though the only object is to gain information, is by no means free from danger. The detachment sent on this occasion was repeatedly attacked by parties of French and Indians, and they lost in the course of the expedition nearly fifty men and several officers.

Attack at the Mouth of the Montmorency

Finding no crossing place up the river, General Wolfe determined to attack the French lines by crossing the Montmorency at its mouth, where the waters flowed over a wide beach of sand, in a shallow current which was fordable at low tide. Two brigades were to cross this ford at midnight. At the same time a large number of men were to be sent on shore in boats from the fleet, and a man-of-war, brought up near, was to cannonade the French works on the land.

This deep-laid plain was, however, destined not to succeed. The boats got entangled among the rocks, and the men in them were detained a long time. Two transports fell aground, too, and finally had to be set on fire. In a word, the attempt was a failure, and the English were obliged to retreat, with a loss of four hundred men.

SICKNESS OF GENERAL WOLFE

The fatigues and exposures incident to these operations, together with the anxiety of mind and bitter disappointments which resulted from the failure of them, brought upon General Wolfe the return of a malady to which he was subject, and for a time almost incapacitated him for action. In this emergency he wrote a letter to the three principal officers under his command—the brigadier-generals Moncton, Townsend and Murray—asking their opinion in respect to what it was best to do. After consultation they wrote a reply, in which they expressed the opinion that it would be better to abandon the attempt to attack Quebec from below, and to pass with the ships above the town and advance upon it in that direction. General Wolfe approved of this suggestion, and it was at once determined to adopt the plan proposed.

PREPARATIONS FOR CARRYING THE NEW PLAN INTO EFFECT

The sickness of General Wolfe and the time consumed in making the necessary preparations for changing the mode of attack caused a delay of many weeks, and it was near the middle of September before things were in readiness for the new assault upon the town to be made from up the river. During this interval General Wolfe took every possible precaution to prevent his new designs from being suspected by the enemy. He sent a considerable number of his ships above the town and anchored them there. This movement, of course, the French could not but observe, but in order to prevent their attention from being particularly attracted to it he sent the vessels up a few at a time, and brought troops to them as much as possible by stealth and in the night, or by a roundabout way over land. He also kept everything as quiet as possible on board the ships. The place where he stationed the ships, too, was quite far up the river, ten or twelve miles beyond Quebec, and at a point where there was no probability that he could have any intention to land.

In the meantime he continued a great deal of pretended preparation below the town. He had boats out making soundings along the shore between the mouths of the St. Charles and the Montmorency, opposite to the French lines, as if he was intending to make a new attempt at landing there, and resorted to a great many other similar devices in order to mislead the enemy in respect to his real intentions.

THE ATTACK

At length, on the night of the 13th of September, all was ready for the attack. Four or five regiments of chosen troops were put on board a fleet of flat-bottomed boats from the vessels up the river, and a little after midnight the boats set out to come down the current. The vessels remained where they were for a short time, until the boats were well underway, and then followed them. Thus the ships and the boats arrived at the intended landing-place—which was about a mile or two above Quebec—at nearly the same time. The ships could thus cover the landing of the troops by throwing shot and shell over the bank and keeping the ground clear there, in case their attempt should be discovered, and the enemy should attempt to resist them.

CURIOUS COINCIDENCE

It may seem strange that these boats should be able to pass down the river, even in the night, without attracting the attention of the French sentries that would naturally be placed along the shore. Indeed, it was expected that they would be observed, and that the alarm would be given, but it was hoped that the boats would nevertheless be able to reach the landing place before any considerable body of troops could be brought up to oppose them. It so happened, however, that the French, who were in great distress for want of provisions, expected a convoy of their own boats to come down the river that night with supplies. This was, of course, a very dangerous undertaking, but it was hoped that the boats might succeed in passing the English ships in the dark by keeping near the shore, and the necessities of the garrison were so great that it was thought best to make the attempt.

Now by great good fortune General Wolfe learned these facts from two deserters who came off to the ships a day or two before the attempt was made. The deserters also communicated the password or countersign which had been given to the men in the French boats, by which they were to make themselves known to the sentries along the banks. Accordingly General Wolfe had only to give this countersign to his men, and thus the sentries, when they perceived and challenged them, and obtained the countersign in reply, supposed that they were their friends bringing reinforcements and provisions, and allowed them to pass without giving any alarm.

CALMNESS AND COMPOSURE OF GENERAL WOLFE

The utmost stillness was observed on board the boats while they were descending the river, and every other precaution was taken to attract the attention of the sentinels on the shore as little as possible, and thus the little fleet passed most of the pickets without being observed. A young midshipman, who was on board the boat which conveyed Wolfe himself, and who afterward became a man of distinction in England, relates that during the passage Wolfe occupied the minds of those who were with him in his boat, by repeating to them in a low and scarcely audible tone of voice, the whole of Gray's Elegy in a Country Churchyard, beginning:

The curfew tolls the knell of parting day.

If his object in doing this was to divert the thoughts of his men from the desperate perils they were about to encounter, and to relieve the feelings of solemnity and awe so naturally excited by the darkness, the solitude, and the impending danger, we might almost suppose he would have omitted the stanza containing the line:

The paths of glory lead but to the grave.

The men listened with very deep interest to the recitation of the lines, and after coming to the end of them the general expressed his great admiration of them, and added that he would rather have been the author of those lines than to take Quebec.

The Landing

At length the boats reached the place which had been selected for the landing. It was now about an hour before daybreak. There was a beach at the margin of the water, with a steep and densely wooded bank ascending to the cliffs above. There was only one path up the ascent. Wolfe himself was the first to leap on shore, and when he saw how steep the declivity was, and how encumbered it was with rocks, trees and bushes, he said to an officer near him, who was to lead the advance:

"I doubt if you will get up, but you must do what you can."

The path was guarded by a small body of men that were stationed near the top of it, on the high ground above. On the command being given the English soldiers rushed up the acclivity, some making their way by the path, and others scrambling as they could among the trees and bushes. The guard at the top of the path was soon overpowered, and then there was no farther opposition to the ascent of the bank by the men. In the meantime, the boats having discharged their loads went back to the ships for more men, and thus in a short time a large force succeeded in reaching the heights, and were there soon disposed in order of battle.

Advance of the French to Meet the Enemy

In the meantime the alarm had spread rapidly to all the French posts on that side of the city, and bodies of troops were seen coming

Landing under the cliff.

in every direction to meet the invaders. The commander, Montcalm, sent forward a large number of Indians into the woods in front of the ground occupied by the English, to commence firing upon them, in order to harass them and keep them back until the main body should arrive. The English waited patiently until the main body came. They then pressed forward to attack them and a long and desperate conflict ensued.

THE BATTLE

It would be painful to dwell upon the horrid incidents of a cruel and bloody contest like this where thousands of men are employed for hours in slaughtering one another, the scene being made the more frightful by the roar of cannon, the sharp rattling of musketry, the demoniac yells of savages, and the piteous moans or agonizing shrieks of the wounded and dying. It is sufficient for our purpose to say that the English were completely victorious. The French were everywhere routed and driven from the field, and thus the way was left open for the advance of the English to Quebec, only a mile or two distant, and on that side almost wholly undefended.

DEATH OF BOTH THE GENERALS

One among the many remarkable circumstances which combine to render this battle so famous in history as it has become, is the fact that both the commanding generals were slain. Both, too, seem to have died rejoicing. General Wolfe, the English commander, after having been for many months continually harassed by disappointment, sickness, vexatious failures, and gloomy forebodings, found at last that the success of the grand expedition, which had been organized at such an expense of men and money, and intrusted to his charge, and which he had brought across the Atlantic, and watched over with so much anxiety during the long months of the summer, was now fully and unquestionably secured. When he was told, after receiving his wound, and while he was gasping for breath, that the French were flying from the field, he said he died content, and almost immediately expired.

The Marquis of Montcalm, on the other hand, when told that his wound was mortal, said he was glad that it was so. He rejoiced that he was not to live to witness the surrender of Quebec.

AFTER THE BATTLE

By the death of General Wolfe the command of the English forces devolved upon General Townshend. He did not immediately advance upon Quebec, but devoted his attention first to the work of strengthening and securing the position which had already been gained, and making preparations for a more effectual attack upon the city when the proper time should arrive. He accordingly threw up intrenchments around his camp, and brought on additional reinforcements from the ships, and made a good road up the bank, by means of which the men drew up artillery, ammunition and supplies. He also began to erect batteries from which the city might be cannonaded. Some of these batteries were so placed as to command the avenues of approach to the town, so as to prevent the inhabitants and the garrison from receiving any fresh supplies of provision from the country.

MESSAGE FROM THE GOVERNOR

The governor of the city, whose name was De Ramsey, watched these proceedings very anxiously for several days, until at length, being convinced that no means of escape were left to him from the toils which were being drawn more and more tightly around him, he determined on offering to surrender, provided he could make honorable terms with the enemy.

Accordingly, on the 17th day of September, four days after the battle, and only a short time before the new batteries would be ready to open upon the city, he sent out a flag of truce, with proposals to surrender the city on certain conditions. The conditions which he proposed, together with the answers of the English general, were substantially as follows:

Proposed Capitulation

Article 1.—Monsieur De Ramsey requires that in giving up the city the garrison shall be allowed to retire with honor, and to take with them their arms, baggage, and six pieces of cannon, and to march without molestation by the shortest road to the main body of the French army.

The answer was that the garrison could not be allowed to join the French army. They would be permitted to march out of the city with the honors of war—taking their arms and baggage, with drums beating, lighted matches, and two pieces of cannon. They would, however, be required to be embarked as soon as possible, under supervision of the English army, on board ships which would convey them to the first port in France.

Article 2.—That the inhabitants of the town shall retain possession of their houses, goods, and all their privileges undisturbed.

Answer. Granted, provided they lay down their arms.

Article 3.—That the inhabitants shall not be molested in any way on account of their having borne arms in defense of the town, as they had been compelled to do so.

Granted.

Article 4.—That the effects of such officers or inhabitants as might be absent from the town shall not be disturbed.

Granted.

Article 5.—That the inhabitants shall not be removed from the town, nor be compelled to quit their houses, until their condition shall be settled by a treaty between the kings of England and France.

Granted.

Article 6.—That the exercise of the Catholic religion shall be preserved; that the houses of the clergy, particularly the residence of the bishop of Quebec, and all the convents, monasteries, and churches shall be protected; and the bishop allowed to remain and exercise freely all his episcopal functions, in such manner as he shall think fit, until a treaty shall be made.

Granted.

These were the principal articles. There were a few others relating to the care of the sick and wounded, and to measures of precaution to be taken to guard against any injury to the town, and more especially to the churches and monasteries, by the soldiers, at the time of taking possession.

The English general assented to all these proposals, as he did substantially to all the articles except the first, which claimed permission for the garrison to go and join the main French army, which was now up the river in the direction of Montreal. This the English general would not allow, but insisted on putting them on board ships and sending them home to France, so as effectually to prevent their taking any farther part in the contest.

THE ULTIMATUM

The messengers who came with the flag of truce bringing the proposals of the governor, waited for their answer, and took it back with them that same day. They were directed to inform the governor of Quebec that unless he sent back word within four hours that he would give up the town, on the terms signified in the answer, the English general would listen to no further proposals, but would proceed at once to take the town by storm.

THE TOWN SURRENDERED

The governor decided to comply, and the articles of capitulation were accordingly signed by both parties. Immediately afterward an English officer was sent with three companies of grenadiers to take possession of the upper town, while a large body of seamen from the ships landed on the beach below and took possession of the lower town.

FURTHER CONTINUANCE OF THE WAR

The surrender of Quebec by no means finished the war in Canada. The French still had a large army in the field, and the military operations of the two powers against each other continued for some years. The French at one time made an attempt to recover possession of Quebec. But they did not succeed.

In fact they did not succeed at all in any of their attempts to resist the progress of the English arms. They were gradually driven back from one position to another, until at length what remained of their army was hemmed in at Montreal, and obliged to surrender, and thus the whole of Canada fell into English hands.

CHAPTER X
PONTIAC

CESSION OF CANADA TO THE ENGLISH

A s has already been stated, it was in the year 1759 that Quebec was captured by the English army under General Wolfe, by the battle on the heights of Abraham, as related in the last chapter. But, although this city was by far the strongest and most important place in the French possessions, the fall of it did not end the war. The resistance of the French, as stated in the close of the last chapter, was continued in and around Montreal. They were at length defeated there also, but the struggle did not entirely cease until the establishment of peace between the two parent countries in Europe, which event took place in the year 1763. In settling the terms of this peace it was agreed that the French should cede to the English government all their possessions in North America. The Canadas, Nova Scotia, and New Brunswick were thus formally transferred to the British crown, and they have continued to be provinces of the British empire to the present day.

TAKING POSSESSION OF THE COUNTRY

The cession of the territory by the French did not, however, at once give the English possession of the country, especially of the western portion, where many French forts and trading houses had been established at important and commanding points in the Indian country, along the margins of the lakes and rivers. The French officers in command of these stations were, of course, ready at once to surrender them, but the Indians themselves might be expected to have something to say on the subject of such a transfer. The English appear to have apprehended some difficulty on this point, and they determined to do all in their power to avoid it. It was, however, necessary to take formal possession of the various posts, and as soon as peace was concluded, an officer named Major Rogers was sent with a detachment of troops to perform this duty.

Pontiac

Major Rogers met with no immediate opposition in his first advance into the Indian territory. On the contrary, he was received in rather a friendly manner by the Indians whom he encountered, and especially by Pontiac, one of the most powerful and renowned of the native chieftains. Pontiac, however, soon afterward organized a very extended conspiracy and combination among the northwestern Indians, for the purpose of expelling the English from their country, and recovering possession of it for themselves. This led to a very bloody war. It was the last of the struggles in which the English colonies were engaged previous to the outbreak of the Revolution, and will accordingly form the subject of the closing chapter of this volume.

First Interview with Pontiac

The first acquaintance that the English formed with Pontiac was on the occasion of the march of Major Rogers into the Indian country, to take possession of the French forts and trading houses there. While on the way he was met one day by a party of Indian chieftains and warriors, who stated to him that they had been sent forward by their grand sachem Pontiac, who, as they said, was king and lord of the whole country which the English troops were entering, and who was coming to meet them, and to have an interview with the commander; and in the meantime, they added, his orders were that Major Rogers should halt and remain where he was until Pontiac should come up.

Major Rogers accordingly halted his troops and encamped, to await Pontiac's arrival. Before long he came. He advanced into the English camp, surrounded and followed by a band of chieftains and warriors, and assuming an air of majesty and princely grandeur. After the first salutation he demanded, somewhat sternly, what the occasion was of the English officer coming into *his* country, at the head of an armed force, and why he had presumed to do so without first obtaining permission from him.

MODERATION OF MAJOR ROGERS

Major Rogers was a man of too much sagacity and self-possession to take offence at this summons. He assumed a very friendly tone and manner, and endeavored by every means in his power to avoid awakening Pontiac's hostility. He told him that in coming into the country the English were actuated by no hostile or even by any unfriendly intentions toward the Indians. On the contrary, they wished to continue on the most amicable terms with them—their chief design in wishing to come into the country at all being to carry on a friendly trade and commerce with them, which would be of equal advantage to both parties. The military force which he was leading, Major Rogers said, was not intended to act against the Indians in any sense whatever, but only to take possession of the posts and strongholds of the French, a nation that the English were desirous of dispossessing mainly on account of the influence they had exerted on the minds of the Indians, in preventing a good understanding between them and their true friend and father the king of Great Britain.

PONTIAC'S DECISION

Pontiac seems to have been on the whole favorably impressed with the view of the case which Major Rogers so adroitly presented. He said he would consider the subject and make known his decision on the following morning, and in the meantime the English troops must remain where they were, without attempting to resume their march;— or, as he expressed it, "I shall stand in the path that you are walking until the morning."

In the morning Pontiac manifested a desire to take a favorable view of the question, and to allow the English to proceed. Major Rogers made every effort to confirm and strengthen this good disposition on the part of the savage potentate, and he seems to have succeeded very well. Various negotiations followed, accompanied

155

by presents of wampum, beads, guns, and other such objects as are used as tokens and pledges of friendship on such occasions, and also by many smokings of the calumet or pipe of peace; and agreements and treaties were made, more or less vague and uncertain in their character, and in some degree susceptible of a double interpretation, as was usually the case in respect to treaties between the English and the Indians—the English generally considering these treaties as *deeds of cession* on the part of the Indians, by which the jurisdiction over the country was in some sense conveyed to the newcomers, while the Indians regarded them as only treaties of amity and alliance between equal sovereigns.

Indeed, it was the general policy of the Europeans in all cases to be satisfied with any agreement or convention with the Indians which would enable them to get into their country and establish themselves in the possession of the important points, knowing well that their strength at these points would very rapidly increase, and that they could extend their claims and pretensions afterward, as occasion should require.

IDEAS AND INTENTIONS OF PONTIAC

In this case Pontiac supposed that he was very careful to guard all his rights as sovereign of the country. He agreed to allow the English troops to advance, and even promised to accompany and aid them; but it was only with a view to their assuming the position which the French were going to surrender, namely that of allies of the Indians admitted within their territory for purposes of trade. He even seemed disposed to make the relation of the English government to his own less near and intimate than that of the French had been. In their diplomatic covenants the king of the French had been styled their *father*. Pontiac, however, gave the king of England only the title of *uncle*—a distinction which in his eyes was probably one of considerable importance—though one to which, as it would seem, Major Rogers paid very little attention. All that it was of any moment for him to secure was the means of going forward and taking possession of Detroit and the other ports on the northwestern frontier without any obstruction.

THE ENGLISH TAKE POSSESSION

Accordingly, the troops under Major Rogers moved on, and in due time the English were installed in possession of the posts and trading houses which had been established by the French in all the northwestern territory, from Niagara westward to the Mississippi, and southward to, and even beyond the Ohio.

These posts were generally established at commanding positions on the lakes and on the great rivers for which the whole region is so remarkable. The country is generally very level, so that the rivers are in most cases deep and still, while the dense forests, which in general occupied the land in those days, rendered land transportation as inconvenient and difficult, as conveyance by canoes upon the water was easy and safe. The possession of these commanding points, which generally occupied the sites upon which great towns have since sprung up—gave the power that held them the control substantially of the whole country.

PONTIAC CHANGES HIS POLICY

It was not long, however, before Pontiac began to feel uneasy in respect to the progress that the English were making in what he considered his country. For some time he revolved the subject in his mind and watched anxiously the progress of events, until, at length, he came to the conclusion that he had made a great mistake in aiding the English to get possession of the land, that by so doing he had introduced an enemy that was rapidly extending his power, and would soon wholly overwhelm the natives, unless they united to resist and expel him. He finally concluded to form a grand league among all the various tribes scattered over the northwestern country, for making a general attack upon the English settlements and destroying them all at a single blow.

PROGRESS OF THE CONSPIRACY

Pontiac spent some time in visiting the sachems of the different tribes, and in conversing with the various chieftains and warriors, and he found them everywhere very ready to adopt his views. At length a grand council was called to mature the plans of action. This council was held secretly. All the leading sachems were present, and after the usual deliberations had been held, according to the Indian custom on such occasions, the plans were formed and the instructions given.

PRETENDED REVELATION FROM HEAVEN

At this council Pontiac solemnly informed the assembly that in acting as he had done he was following the directions of the Great Spirit, who had appeared to a certain Delaware Indian, and declared His will that the English should be expelled, and had moreover given specific instructions in respect to the measures to be adopted for the accomplishment of the object. The Great Spirit, he said, appeared angry and indignant, and demanded why the Indians suffered the white men to come among them.

"Why," said the Great Spirit, as Pontiac stated in his speech, "Why do you allow these red dogs," referring to the English soldiers, whose uniform in those days was red, "to come into your country, and take away from you the land which I have given you. Drive them away! Drive them away. If you get into difficulty or distress by so doing I will help you."

CONCERTED ATTACK UPON THE ENGLISH STATIONS

The plan which was adopted was to organize a great number of distinct and independent expeditions throughout all the country, and then, on a preconcerted day, to attack simultaneously all the stations of the English in every part of the northwestern territory. We have not remaining space in this volume to give a full account of the manner in which this plan was carried into effect. It is sufficient to say that most efficient preparations were made—and in the most wily and secret manner—for organizing the several expeditions, and at the appointed time the attacks were made, all nearly on the same day. The English garrisons were everywhere taken entirely by surprise. In some cases they succeeded in defending their posts and in beating off the assailants, but *nine* of the stations were captured.

Arrangements were made, too, for intercepting all the various parties of English traders that were on their way in different parts of the country, to and from the various forts. In this way great numbers of men were made prisoners, and a large quantity of goods was captured.

STRATAGEMS

In the cases in which the Indians succeeded in getting possession of the forts, they generally accomplished their purpose more by stratagem than by force. They would send to a trading house or station one or two squaws, or Indian travelers, apparently worn out with the fatigue of a long journey, to beg a shelter for the night, and then the persons so received would open the gates at midnight and let their confederates come in. At one place a woman came to the gates of a blockhouse apparently in a state of great terror and distress, and implored the commander of it to come out with a small party to rescue a man in the woods not far off, who had been wounded and was dying. The commander, not suspecting any treachery, went with the woman without any hesitation. He and his men were led into an ambuscade and shot; and then the Indians, making a sudden rush at the blockhouse, forced their way in and overwhelmed the little garrison.

THE MACKINAW GAME OF BALL

The most remarkable of the stratagems adopted by the Indians to gain admission to these strongholds was the one adopted at Mackinaw, a place situated on the southern side of the strait that connects lakes Huron and Michigan. The original Indian name of this post was Michilimackinac, but in modern times the word has been shortened to Mackinaw. The station consisted in those days of a blockhouse or fort, and a village of about thirty houses, the whole inclosed in a high and strong palisade. The space included within the inclosure comprised about two acres.

The Indians came in large numbers, but apparently in a very peaceable manner, and encamped near the fort. Here, after engaging in various festivities, which the people of the fort and village witnessed as spectators, they finally proposed to have on a certain day, a grand game after their fashion, which was played with a ball. There were men of two tribes present, namely, Chippewas and Sacs. These formed the two parties to the game, the object being to see which of the tribes would beat the other. The game was to be played by setting two bounds half a mile or more apart, and then placing the ball upon the ground in the middle between them, when the two parties were at once to assail it, armed with bats formed of stout sticks cut from the forests, and each party was to endeavor to knock the ball toward the antagonist's bound. Of course the party which should first succeed in driving the ball beyond the opposite bound were to be considered the victors.

DESIGN OF THE INDIANS

Of course a game like this, played by Indian warriors, was likely to result in some very rough work, such as Englishmen of the lower classes take special pleasure in witnessing. Parties of savages rushing up from opposite sides, aiming blows with heavy clubs at a ball lying on the ground between them, and incited by rivalry and pride to surpass each other, might be expected to lead to serious accidents and personal conflicts, and, perhaps, even to a general fight. Of course the garrison, and the people generally of the village, were expected to take great interest in coming out to witness the game, by which means the post would be left in some measure unguarded, and the savages might hope to rush in and take possession of it.

SUCCESS OF THE STRATAGEM

The Indians did all in their power to interest the soldiers and the men living in the village, in the proposed game, by making great preparations for it, and inviting them particularly to come out and see it. In due time the game was commenced. After it was well underway the Indians contrived gradually to work the ball along in the direction of the palisade, not far from the entrance, and then, as if by accident, to knock it over within the inclosure. They then all with one accord made a rush toward the entrance, as if to go in and recover the ball. No sufficient resistance was offered, and several hundred savages made their way in. As soon as they found themselves once within the inclosure they abandoned all thoughts of the ball, and drawing forth concealed weapons they immediately rushed upon the people, and began to murder indiscriminately all that came in their way. The soldiers, who had not the least suspicion of what was coming, were taken entirely off their guard, and were easily overpowered.

DETROIT

The most important of all the establishments which the French had made in the northwest territory, was the settlement at Detroit. The place was very important, not only on account of its position—being situated at the entrance of Lake Huron, and thus commanding the main avenue of approach to the three great western lakes—but also on account of the size of the place, and the very large accumulation of property stored there, which amounted at this time, it was said, to between two and three million dollars. These stores consisted of valuable furs brought in from the various trading stations, and also of large stocks of merchandise of various kinds, brought there for the purpose of trade with the Indians, and also to supply the wants of the European settlers.

CONSTRUCTION OF THE PLACE

The place consisted of a sort of fortification with a number of log-houses, forming a small village, inclosed in it. The whole was surrounded by a very high and solid fence called a stockade, which was formed of long and stout posts set close together in the ground. At the corners of this inclosure, and over the gates, there were built blockhouses, with platforms above, on which cannon were mounted.

The log-houses were in the center. All around the group of houses, and between them and the stockade, was an open space, which served as a street, and also as a place for mustering and training the soldiers.

PLAN OF ATTACK CONCERTED BY THE INDIANS

The plan which the Indians formed for getting possession of this place involved, as usual, a cunning stratagem. Their project was to come in large numbers and encamp in the vicinity of the place, as they were often accustomed to do in times of peace, and then to contrive under some pretext to gain admission for a certain number of warriors secretly armed, within the gates, in hopes by so doing of being able to surprise and overpower the garrison. These men were to be provided with rifles which had been shortened by being sawed off, so that they could conceal them entirely from view by hiding them under their blankets.

DISCOVERY OF THE PLOT

This plan might, perhaps, have succeeded had it not been accidentally, or, at any rate, unintentionally betrayed. Major Gladwin was the name of the commander of the fort, and he had always been very honorable in all his dealings with the Indians, and very kind to them. It seems he had employed an Indian woman to make him a pair of moccasins, and had given her a valuable fur to make them of. In due time the woman brought home the moccasins to the fort, and also the portion of the fur that was left over. Major Gladwin liked the work very much. He paid the woman generously for the pair of moccasins that she had made, and directed her to take back the rest of the fur—which was an elk skin—and make it all up into moccasins of the same kind.

The woman took the fur and went out; but she lingered about the door, and seemed uneasy. A servant asked her whether she was waiting for anything, but he could not get any satisfactory answer. Presently the major coming out, saw her, and asked her if there was anything that she wanted. She said she did not wish to take away the fur, for if she did she should not be able to bring it back again; and she did not wish to make the major lose it, since he had been so kind to her.

Major Gladwin's attention was at once strongly arrested. He suspected that something unusual was about to occur, and after questioning the woman closely he ascertained the truth in respect to the attack upon the fort which the Indians were planting.

THE PLOT DEFEATED

Of course Major Gladwin made thorough preparations for receiving the Indian warriors when they should come. He did not refuse them admittance, but as soon as they were fairly within the inclosure and under his control, the drums beat to arms, and the whole garrison came suddenly forth and surrounded them, with bayonets fixed and muskets loaded. Major Gladwin then immediately walked up to Pontiac, lifted up his blanket, and brought to view the rifle which was hidden beneath it.

He then reproached the Indians with their faithlessness and perfidy, and ordered them all out of the fort. They retired confounded, but at once prepared for open war.

They, of course, had no artillery with which they might hope to make a breach in the stockade, and so they contented themselves with surrounding the place and firing upon it incessantly from the best places of shelter that they could find.

It seems there were several out-buildings of different kinds in the neighborhood, outside of the stockade, and these furnished protection to the assailants until the English set them on fire, firing red-hot spikes into them from the cannons on the platforms, and thus burned the Indians out of them. The Indians were in this way driven farther back, but they still kept up so continual a firing day and night, that the garrison were at length almost entirely exhausted by want of sleep and incessant labor.

ATTEMPTS TO RELIEVE THE GARRISON

Several attempts were made at different times to send relief to the garrison. In one instance the reinforcements came in a fleet of boats, but just before they reached the place, the party stopped as usual at night to encamp upon the shore, and in the morning they were surprised by the Indians, and the whole party, boats and all, were captured.

The Indians then compelled the boatmen and soldiers, after first disarming them, to take their places in the boats and go on as if nothing had happened, putting, however, two Indians, well-armed, into each boat, to guard them, and also following them with the rest of their force in detachments, through the bushes along the shore, to watch them and fire upon them if any of the men should attempt to make any resistance. They hoped in this manner to advance by stealth near enough to the town to surprise and capture an armed sloop which lay in the river opposite to it.

But the plan did not succeed. The English soldiers in one of the boats rose upon the guards at the imminent risk of their lives, upon which they were immediately fired at, both by the guards and by the Indians on the shore. The Englishmen in the boat then leaped into the water. One was drowned, but the rest escaped to the schooner. This affair gave the alarm, and the schooner immediately began to fire upon the Indians in the woods, who were all thus driven away. The other boats, however, were immediately paddled to the shore by the Indian guards that had been stationed in them, and the English prisoners were all murdered.

END OF THE WAR

But we cannot give in detail the history of the siege, nor of the other events connected with the war. It is sufficient to say that the English resisted all these attacks with so much vigor, and received in process of time such heavy reinforcements from the eastward, that the Indians at length became weary of the contest, and peace was restored.

CONCLUSION

When the war with Pontiac and his allies was ended, and the western and northwestern Indians, abandoning all idea of expelling the English from their country, returned to their usual avocations, the country was once more at peace, and all the settlements of European origin on the Atlantic seaboard, and along the line of the great lakes and western rivers to the Mississippi, as far north and west as the white man had penetrated, and southward almost to the Gulf of Mexico, were firmly, and to all appearance permanently, established under English sway. In less than ten years from this time, however, subjects of dissension arose between these colonies and the mother country, which led finally to a revolution. The origin and nature of these dissensions, and the revolt which sprang from them, will form the subject of the next volume of this series.

THE END.

Made in the USA
Middletown, DE
28 November 2022

16276027R00099